On
the Trail

50 YEARS OF ENGAGING WITH NATURE

WRITTEN BY:

Anthea Farr	Anne Gosse	Sheila Puls
Lilianne Fuller	Phil Henderson	Joanne Rosenthal
Lisa Dreves	Gareth Pugh	Nora Truman
John Gordon	Bob Puls	

Glen R Ryder
-1979-
Ruffed Grouse

We acknowledge with gratitude that we operate on the unceded, sovereign Indigenous lands of the Stó:lō Coast Salish Peoples. These include territories of the q'ʷa:n̓ƛ̓ən̓ (Kwantlen), q̓ic̓əy̓ (Katzie), Máthxwi (Matsqui), and se'mya'me (Semiahmoo) First Nations.

Cataloguing data available from Library and Archives Canada
978-0-88839-759-1 [paperback]
978-0-88839-757-7 [epub]

Illustrations and photographs are copyrighted by the artist or the Publisher.
Cover/Interior Design: Emily Morton
Front Cover Photo: Milaster Passive Park by Bob Puls
Back Cover Photo: Douglas Squirrel at Campbell Valley Park by Anthea Farr

Hancock House acknowledges the support of the Government of Canada through the
Canada Book Fund and the Canada Council for the Arts, and of the Province of British Columbia
through the British Columbia Arts Council and the Book Publishing Tax Credit.

Proudly Printed & Bound in Canada.
This book has been printed on Ancient Forest Friendly and 100% recycled
paper fiber, certified by the Forest Stewardship Council®.

The Langley Field Naturalists gratefully acknowledge the support of the BC Naturalist's
Foundation, BC Nature, emcreative Graphic Design and the City of Langley.

Published simultaneously in Canada and the United States by

HANCOCK HOUSE PUBLISHERS LTD.
19313 Zero Avenue, Surrey, B.C. Canada V3Z 9R9
#104-4550 Birch Bay-Lynden Rd, Blaine, WA, U.S.A. 98230-9436
(800) 938-1114   Fax (800) 983-2262
www.hancockhouse.com   info@hancockhouse.com

*Hancock House gratefully acknowledges the Halkomelem Speaking Peoples whose
unceded, shared and asserted traditional territories our offices reside upon.*

Supported by the Province of British Columbia

CONTENTS

INTRODUCTION

Over the past 50 years, Langley has experienced rapid growth and many changes. Cow pastures have been replaced by condos and commercial hubs. Some of us still remember when Gibson's Cattle Auction was located on the main street of Langley City.

Irene Pearce Trail. Photo: Anthea Farr

This rapid development has resulted in a shrinking of natural areas and green space. Fifty years ago, the Langley Field Naturalists Society (LFN) formed to *know nature and to keep nature worth knowing.*

This book is a celebration of the nature that still exists in Langley, thanks in part to the work of LFN members. We reveal how we kept our group together and thriving for 50 years: the activities and the individuals. Also revealed are the secrets of how we saved or enriched natural areas. A half century of successes and failures has taught us much.

On the Trail could also be viewed as a call to action. The next 50 years will not be easy. Like the LFN, all who care about nature will need to make choices that serve us well in the sometimes fickle, sometimes ferocious, face of climate change. Habitat loss caused by human activities will also be an ongoing challenge. Every gram of resolve and effort will be needed to save at-risk species, threatened habitats and our own wellbeing.

Luckily, naturalist societies offer ways to both connect with and to care for nature. These pages contain examples of how we did this. Perhaps our successes will inspire others to achieve similar results, in other regions of the province or beyond.

We hope you enjoy this stroll back in time, looking at the trails we have travelled, literally and figuratively. Langley still has wonderfully diverse flora and fauna, if you know where to look.

As ever, the trail ahead beckons.

CHAPTER 1

Early Beginnings: Sowing and Nurturing

by Phil Henderson

> ## "The question is not what you look at, but what you see."
>
> **– HENRY DAVID THOREAU**

Glenn Ryder spent much time in the 1950s and 1960s exploring forests and remnant natural areas in Langley and Surrey, taking detailed notes on the plants and animals he observed. This experience provided him with a unique perspective on their ecological value and the consequences of their loss.

A favourite area for his wildlife investigations was along the Little Campbell River and he realized this important area could be lost if it was not protected. He began to rally support for its conservation by alerting fellow naturalist Al Grass and other concerned citizens sympathetic to the plight of local wildlife and the loss of natural spaces.

This informal group heralded the beginning of the Langley Field Naturalists which wasn't officially formed until 1973. These early years, preceding the establishment of Campbell Valley Regional Park in 1969, were the club's formative years: the years in which like-minded and spirited individuals took up the torch for nature in Langley, a torch Langley Field Naturalists have not relinquished.

Key participants in this early fight were Al Grass, Glenn's dear friend and kindred spirit; Adeline Nicol, a wildflower enthusiast;

Facing: Where are we going? Photo: LFN Archives

Ray Gurr, photographer and City of Surrey Parks employee; Mary Pastrick, a bird enthusiast who became a Langley Field Naturalists' President; John Ellens, a long-time local resident, and others. Adeline Nicol attended most Langley Township Council meetings to alert the Mayor and Council of the day to the importance of the natural areas along the Little Campbell River and the need to protect them.

This small but growing group contacted the media, including John Rogers, a reporter with the Vancouver Sun, and Tony Eberts, a reporter for The Province, who covered stories about the group's fight to conserve the area. Jude Grass, who worked as a naturalist and administrator for Metro Vancouver (formerly the Greater Vancouver Regional District), was deeply involved in BC Nature (then, the Federation of BC Naturalists) and many other conservation organizations. Jude tirelessly promoted nature appreciation and undoubtedly had an unheralded, positive influence on the development of a conservation mindset within Metro Vancouver. Rick Hankin, the Regional Planner for Metro Vancouver, was instrumental in establishing Campbell Valley Regional Park in 1969.

Campbell Valley Regional Park marked the first victory for the group that would become the Langley Field Naturalists. It was the catalyst for the

Glenn Ryder in a Langley forest.
Photo: Trudy Pastrick

On Sept. 29, 1979, MARY PASTRICK participated in an Autumn Nature Walk sponsored by both the Greater Vancouver Regional Parks Department and the Langley Field Naturalists on the occasion of the Grand Opening of Campbell Valley Regional Park.

al Gross
President, L.F.N.

Rich Hankin
Administrater
G.V.R.D. (Parks)

Above: Early boardwalk at Campbell Valley Park. Photo: LFN Archives
Left: Campbell Valley Park certificate. Photo: Anthea Farr

formation of the LFN, bringing more members as existing trails were improved and new trails were built in the newly created park. Glenn Ryder, who had initially brought attention to this important natural area, spent less time there as the number of park visitors increased. He became concerned with visitors who often let their dogs off-leash, which disturbed the wildlife. Glenn preferred exploring nature by himself or in small groups and so became less involved in Langley Field Naturalists' activities, indoors and outdoors, but maintained close ties with club members. He felt a sense of pride in having contributed with Al and Jude and others to a community-wide awareness of the importance of natural spaces and wildlife in Langley. Although he visited the Park less often and avoided the people and the trails as best as he could, it remained an important area to him.

Al fondly recalls Glenn showing him a Red Fox den he had discovered in the park. Together, they began to unveil the park's other little-known natural history wonders, including two orchids—Hooded Ladies' Tresses and Spotted Coralroot—and an aquatic liverwort, all often overlooked, uncommon plants of the Lower Mainland. Glenn included Campbell Valley Regional Park for "Project Screech-Owl," his personal project which involved placing nest boxes across the Fraser Valley to curb the species' decline which he had documented from field observations.

Are we all here yet? Photo: LFN Archives

Al Grass was the club's first president from 1973 to 1974, the only year in which Glenn Ryder was on the Executive, as Director of Programmes. Al set the tone and a standard for the Langley Field Naturalists by promoting an approach to natural history based on exploration and discovery, a philosophy rooted in the early American naturalist Henry David Thoreau's idea that the destination is less important and inspiring than what you see and experience along the way. Al's personal formula for nature appreciation is to inspire people with 10% information (i.e., telling) and 90% inspiration (i.e., seeing and showing, experiencing nature). This became the guiding principle of the Langley Field Naturalists under Al's leadership and influence through the years. Anyone who has had the great pleasure of accompanying Al on one of his walks knows the thrill and value of this approach, more a facet of Al's personality than a learned "teaching method."

In these early days of the Langley Field Naturalists, a special spot in Campbell Valley Regional Park was the 'Listening Bridge', also known as 'Owl Corner', on the south side of the Little Campbell River loop. On one memorable occasion, two groups, one from Langley Field Naturalists and one from Nature Vancouver, ventured into the park to play Western Screech-Owl calls in hopes of eliciting a response, possibly even a sighting. Unbeknownst to one another, each group played their recording, and each group heard a response. Slowly they moved towards the source of their respective responses until the two groups met. No one ever knew whether a 'real' Western Screech-Owl called that evening.

The Langley Field Naturalists grew to about 40 members, a mix of young and old. The club began meetings and talks in the original Langley Community Music School (LCMS) building, a drafty structure of odd geometries on the same property as the

Where's that bird? Photo: LFN Archives

new LCMS building. The first newsletters were produced on a mimeograph machine, a mechanical printing device employing stencils produced on special paper with a ribbon-less typewriter. The goal of the club, as related by Al and Jude Grass, was to inspire people to appreciate the wonderful diversity of nature in the area.

Nature interpretation was the focus of outings and the Langley Field Naturalists initiated studies in which members could actively participate, including a raptor count. The raptor survey was conducted over 26 years by keen participants, including Mary and Herb Pastrick, Dan Rempel, Bill Knowlson and Ray Gurr. In those days, Short-eared Owls and Rough-legged Hawks were regularly observed at the Langley airport.

Projects such as this, regular outings and presentations, the quarterly newsletter, and, unfortunately, the persistent disregard for, and destruction of nature in the two Langleys and neighbouring areas of Surrey, ensured a steady core of members with a fluctuating secondary group of interested participants.

Despite having formed years before, first simply as an informal, unnamed group of naturalists and citizens intent on saving lands along the Little Campbell River and later, in 1973, as the Langley Field Naturalists, the club was not officially registered as a society until February 8, 1980. On that date, the Executive, including President Al Grass and other members of the early group, signed a declaration of incorporation under the Provincial Societies Act.

The stated purposes of the Langley Field Naturalists Society were:

1 To further an interest in natural history,

2 To promote conservation of the environment, and

3 To promote education in natural history.

Anthea Farr at LFN display.
Photo: LFN Archives

Slight amendments to the Society's by-laws were made subsequently, resulting in changes to the descriptions of the duties of the Directors and Officers in 1984 signed by President Anthea Farr, and an increase in the Treasurer's spending limit in 1999 signed by President Rhys Griffiths. Other amendments included periodic changes to the club's address when new presidents were elected.

Membership was not always steady, and even within cohesive groups such as the Langley Field Naturalists, disagreements arise between members with strong opinions about the environment. In the mid-1990s, a significant row occurred over the creation of an island for nesting ducks in the Nicomekl River floodplain south of Brydon Lagoon. Members took sides and several people left the club which threatened its collapse. BC Nature suggested a meeting with the few remaining club members who declared, "this club cannot die!"

Rhys and Annabel Griffiths had recently joined the club and Rhys arranged for a meeting in the library of St. Andrew's Anglican Church in Langley. Six members showed up and the meeting was chaired by Martin McNicholl, the club's most recent President. After that meeting, Rhys took on the roles of Membership and Finance, and Annabel became Secretary. Their appointments were critical to the club's resurrection—a fitting result from a church meeting—and the club has flourished since.

The Langley Field Naturalists was born from the passion of a few who recognized the need for conservation and the importance of following a path of education, inspiration, and periodic confrontation with local politicians.

Barn Owl with prey. Photo: John Gordon

THE LFN LOGO

Almost 50 years ago, the LFN chose a logo depicting a stylized Barn Owl. Langley was more agricultural then, with many old wooden barns providing gaps where an owl could fly in and out. Farmers usually welcomed the Barn Owls, as they kept rodent populations in check.

Still present today, Barn Owls fly low over the fields at night, looking for Townsend's Voles, their favourite prey item. Yet hazards may await, such as collisions with vehicles or poison from pesticides.

Maintaining grassy fields will help to conserve these owls. The flash of a "ghost owl" over a moonlit field is unforgettable—a precious part of Langley's heritage.

CHAPTER 2

People Power: Selected Profiles

Pitch-in along the Nicomekl River in 2008. Photo: Bob Puls

"Never underestimate the power of a small group of committed people to change the world. In fact, it is the only thing that ever has."

— MARGARET MEAD

"I go to nature to be soothed and healed, and to have my senses put in order."

— JOHN BURROUGHS

Both of these quotes could help to explain why people join the LFN. Perhaps it is to enact changes that may help nature or perhaps it is to enjoy nature with a like-minded group. Whatever the reason, each member leaves his or her mark in the Society and contributes in some way, however large or small that may be.

Here we highlight just a few of our past and present members who have contributed much to the club. The selection is somewhat random and leaves out a great many influential members. To all of those, we say "Thank you—you will live on in the LFN archives and will always be remembered and appreciated."

We start with three founding members: Glenn Ryder, Al Grass (& spouse Jude), Mary Pastrick (& spouse Herb). Then we highlight nine more members who joined in later decades. They typify the club's diversity of backgrounds, knowledge, and talents: Dr. Fred Bunnell, Anthea Farr, Rhys & Annabel Griffiths, Dr. Martin McNicholl, Phil Henderson, Roy Yates, and Bob & Sheila Puls.

Glenn Ryder BY PHIL HENDERSON

Glenn Ryder was one of the world's great naturalists.

From about age four to his death at 75 in 2013, Glenn explored nature as often as he could, amassing an estimated 1.4 million field notes of plants and animals from excursions throughout BC and into the Yukon (Campbell and Henderson 2015). Many of these records were from Langley where he spent a good portion of his life living and exploring. Glenn's informative notes, often supplemented with detailed sketches, resulted from his patience in watching animals and thoroughly examining the environment in which they occurred.

In addition to providing information on the occurrence and distribution of species, Glenn provided insight into the lives of animals by documenting behaviour, characteristics of nests and dens, competition between and within species, and the influence

Glenn Ryder inspecting a cut bank along Davidson Creek in the "Old Dominion Sawmill Site", February 20, 2009. Photo: Phil Henderson

and threat of humans. The threat presented by human activities to wildlife and habitat contributed to his drive to understand and protect nature and led to the formation of the Langley Field Naturalists (LFN).

As detailed in Chapter 1 of this book, Glenn's call to conserve what we now know as Campbell Valley Regional Park brought together a group of like-minded naturalists (notably Al Grass) and other citizens concerned about the senseless destruction of important natural areas. That group was the foundation of our club.

In the early years of the LFN, Glenn gave a few talks on natural history and led field trips. However, as membership grew, Glenn participated less frequently in monthly meetings and other club activities and in the later years, before his death in 2013, he did not participate at all. Similarly, after Campbell Valley Regional Park was opened to the public and more people started using the park,

Davidson Creek beaver pond. Sketch: Glenn Ryder

Glenn spent less time there monitoring his owl nest boxes and exploring nature. He preferred solitude.

His explorations of nature in Langley shifted to properties in which few people ventured, such as Mountain View near Fort Langley (Chapter 5), which Glenn called the "Old Dominion Sawmill Site". Long before LFN's official involvement there, Glenn visited the site, conducting inventories of plants and animals and an archaeological survey of the old Dominion Sawmill community. He painstakingly screened countless yards of soil using homemade soil screens to unearth clues to the lives of those who had lived and worked there, including the location and type of buildings that formed this early industrial community.

It was along Davidson Creek, which cuts a deep gully through this property, where Glenn witnessed and documented behaviour previously unknown in the Pacific Water Shrew. A species of conservation concern, it is at the northern limit of its range here in the Lower Mainland. The behaviour, known as caravanning, saw the mother leading a procession of her six young, all holding in their jaws the tail of the one in front of them. This and many other important observations and records were published in *Wildlife Afield*, the journal of the Biodiversity Centre for Wildlife Conservation.

A family of Pacific Water Shrews demonstrating caravanning, a previously undocumented behaviour for this species. The Pacific Water Shrew is a federally and provincially endangered species and the largest shrew in British Columbia. Sketch: Glenn Ryder, June 26, 1977. (Used with permission. Originally presented in Campbell and Henderson; 2013).

Glenn never sought publicity but realized his knowledge could be used for conservation. Before his involvement with the LFN, Glenn attempted to change the attitude of people, to influence and educate the public on the value (and plight) of natural spaces and native organisms in Surrey. He established the "BC Wildlife Patrol" in the 1960s to encourage people to discover and appreciate nature, and from 1969 to 1971 he wrote a weekly column about Surrey's plants and animals in The Surrey Leader, each accompanied by an illustration. He later created fine black and white illustrations for the 50 birds presented in LFN's *Birds of Langley*. Painting was another one of his passions; he produced beautiful, detailed portraits of birds, such as the Northern Saw-whet Owl pictured here.

Glenn never sought attention; he avoided it but liked to know that his efforts as a naturalist were recognized and useful. The Langley Field Naturalists and the Abbotsford-Mission Nature Club (formerly the Central Valley Naturalists) awarded Glenn honorary lifetime memberships for

Top: Saw-whet Owl painting by Glenn Ryder
Bottom: Great Blue Heron illustration by Glenn Ryder

his involvement in those clubs and conservation efforts in those communities.

Mostly Glenn used information and knowledge as a passive tool for education and conservation but there were times when he knew he had to act to confront dishonesty and disrespect. He worked occasionally for environmental consultants which provided money for sustenance and exploration, and a means to have his data work to inform development and conserve nature. In one instance he was dismayed and upset when a large Vancouver consulting firm omitted in their report important information Glenn had provided to them about a development property in Langley. He contacted the local press to publicise this omission and make sure it was considered in the assessment. Today, Glenn's records of rare organisms in the Fraser Valley are still presented occasionally in formal reports, sometimes without reference to their discoverer.

Lisa Dreves of Langley Environmental Partner's Society (LEPS) advocated for and received funding to purchase a map of Glenn's observations in the Township of Langley and the accompanying data. This provided Glenn with some money and the knowledge that the data could be used by LEPS and the Township of Langley to conserve important elements of nature, many unknown to everyone but Glenn.

As well as guiding conservation, such data are also useful for guiding development and restoration activities in the Township. With records going back to the 1950s, some of these natural sites have since been destroyed by land development. Yet, thanks to Glenn's valuable data, other sites such as the Municipal Natural Park (Chapter 5) have been preserved.

Campbell Valley Regional Park. Photo: Anthea Farr

Glenn probably amassed the most complete and detailed collection of natural history notes of anyone in BC, and possibly Canada. He didn't have a high profile, an advanced education, or the desire to enter the public forum or fray, so he never received the same billing as famous contemporary or past naturalists. However, what he accomplished personally and in the service of nature, propels him into that company. His was a solo effort, and his contributions, unpublicized and mostly unrewarded financially, remain a testament to his conviction, discipline, and desire to conserve all native species.

Although Glenn seldom attended LFN club activities, he was crucial to its formation and remained an important member. Through his actions and quiet determination, Glenn demonstrated a Langley Field Naturalist's club ethos: to create change through education, conservation, and the occasional need to fight.

References Cited: Campbell, R.W. and P.S. Henderson. 2013. An old-school naturalist. Glenn Roderick Ryder (1938-2013). Wildlife Afield. Volume 10, Number 2, P. 79-256. July-December 2013. Biodiversity Centre for Wildlife Studies.

Al & Jude Grass BY JOHN GORDON

Around us, leaves are turning colour and a steady stream of Black-capped Chickadees are landing on a nearby feeder. It is a perfect setting to chat with my mentor, Al Grass. A founding member of the Langley Field Naturalists, Al has a vast amount of experience and knowledge.

His career as a Naturalist with British Columbia Parks spanned 30 years. During that period, he worked in many parks throughout the province, leading nature walks as a Park Interpreter. As we chatted, I learned how it all began.

Al grew up in Burnaby in the late nineteen fifties and early sixties. Today he lives in Surrey with his equally well known and accomplished partner, wife, and all-round Naturalist, Jude. Al is quite reticent to talk about any of his achievements or himself for that matter, but he commented that growing up in Burnaby

Jude and Al on the prowl. Photo: John Gordon

was wonderful. "There were more open spaces then, more green-ery," he said. He remembers the older homes on Rumble St., long gone now and replaced by high-rises. "Burnaby, like the rest of the Lower Mainland, has changed beyond recognition," he lamented. As a child, Al spent many hours in the garden helping his father. That is where his interest in nature was nurtured.

"My dad was a devoted gardener. It was there I saw butter-flies and all kinds of other creatures. Afterwards, I would look them up in the Golden Guide books," he said. "If I remember, there were twenty volumes on different subjects. A lot of people got their start that way, me included. Each book was two to three dollars. It wasn't like today where you can look up everything on the internet."

Even in his teens, Al knew he wanted to work outdoors in nature. At that time, there were very few colleges or schools that taught anything about nature and conservation. Today these courses are widely offered at universities and technical schools.

His first day on the job as a Park Interpreter was at the Manning Park Nature House. It was there he fielded questions from visitors. "The most popular question was, *Where is the washroom?*" he said with a chuckle.

When not explaining the different flora and fauna, Al's job was to maintain nature trails, put up information signs and complete other duties to make sure visitors got the most out of their nature excursions. One of his bosses was a famous birder named David Stirling. Stirling was in charge of the field programs at Manning Park and he took Al and others under his wing. Later, Al moved up to Wells Gray Park, then back to Manning, then on to Mount

Seymour Park. "I was lucky to have the opportunity to move around," he said.

While working at Golden Ears Park and Cypress Park, he and Jude organized many successful winter programs. "I was one of the lucky ones who was hired full-time; I got to be a career 'Parkie'," he said. "The programs Jude and I were involved in had safety, park heritage, and natural history components. Finally, it was all rolled into one of our *Jerry's Rangers* programs at Rolley Lake and Golden Ears Park. Helping children to be safe in the forest was very important to us," he added.

Al's role as a Park Interpreter was to take the science and convert it into what park users and children could understand. "You want to inspire people who can continue on and learn," he said. "Park interpretation is 10% information and 90% inspiration." Over the years, he has written hundreds of articles

Al Grass with a Bear Hair Lichen moustache. Photo: Bob Puls

and pamphlets and has had many photographs published. His favourite pamphlet was *Campground Critters*.

He feels that it is hard for youngsters today, with so many other distractions such as computers and television, but he is heartened by the success of groups like NatureKids and the British Columbia Field Ornithologists' Young Birders program. Over the years, Al has been able to inspire young people to appreciate and, most importantly, to study nature. "Some of them have even become professors," he said proudly.

Jude and Al met while looking for owls on a Nature Vancouver field trip in Campbell Valley Park. Both were members of Nature Vancouver but had never met. Jude was still in high school but had taken some nature courses. On this owl walk, there were two groups coming from different directions. Al was in one group (led by John Toochin) and Jude was in another. They met and the rest, they say, "is history".

In 1972, Jude and Al were married in an outdoor ceremony in the woods at Mount Seymour by a minister who

Top: Jude Grass.
Photo: John Gordon
Bottom: Ken Kennedy
and the Grasses.
Photo: Anne Gosse

was an avid birder and went by the name of Rev Finch. A few years later, Jude began working for Metro Vancouver Parks, leading interpreter courses, training, and putting programs together for the community. At Campbell Valley Park's Nature House, both Jude and Al were involved in hundreds of school programs through the eighties and nineties.

It has always been Al's philosophy not only to name things but to learn about their ecological background. "When you see a bird, for example—a waxwing feeding on Cascara, people might wonder what that bird is doing; that's the kind of knowledge I want to pass along," he said. "Getting a good list of birds is one thing but we also want to know how the birds live; that's what I enjoy. Each one of our walks we hope someone goes away with knowledge they didn't originally have."

Thousands have taken Al's walks and been enthralled by his easy-going teaching method and deep understanding of the natural world and how it works. The couple's vision was to pass on as much knowledge as possible to those following behind. This has certainly come to pass; they have left a trail of footsteps that will continue to inspire.

EDITOR'S NOTE
Al and Jude both served on the LFN executive for a dazzling number of years. As well as being the club's first President, Al also served later as Field Trip Coordinator. Jude also served as President and Field Trip Coordinator, as well as the club's Program Convener. We are immensely grateful to both of them.

Mary Pastrick

BY ANTHEA FARR

Mary Pastrick, her husband, Herb, and their daughters, especially Trudy, could be viewed as being the "heart" of the LFN in its early decades. Mary's knowledge and love of nature won wide respect from all of the naturalists who knew her. She was one of the province's main contributors to the BC Nest Records Scheme, and she and Herb faithfully maintained their own bluebird nest box trail near Princeton. The Pastricks' acreage in Langley was a haven for birds, deer and other wildlife. Not surprisingly, Mary's farmhouse kitchen was a haven for naturalists.

Whenever she went on nature walks, Mary kept notes on the species she saw or heard. This habit, common among many naturalists, can yield big dividends. Mary's list of birds, from visits to a sewage lagoon over many years, greatly helped LFN's efforts to establish it as a nature park (Brydon Lagoon). Mary's notes also provided valuable reference material for LFN's *Plants of Langley* book, which she co-authored, and LFN's earlier book, *Birds of Langley*.

Mary served in a variety of positions, including President, during her many active years in the Langley Field Naturalists. Willingly and cheerfully, she also donated her time and talents

Mary Pastrick recording birds at Forslunds. Photo: LFN Archives

to club projects. She was an integral part of the early work conducted at Brydon Lagoon and at the Forslund-Watson Wildlife Area, as well as being a key participant in LFN's long-term Raptor Count.

Whether the endeavour was decorating a Christmas tree for the birds outside the Langley Centennial Museum, taking a group of school children on a nature walk, or manning LFN's booth at a busy shopping mall, Mary always volunteered and gave her best. She was one of those rare, multi-faceted naturalists, delighted as much by a mushroom or a wildflower as she was by an owl or a fawn, with the added gift of being able to easily share such joy with others.

Black-tailed Deer. Photo: Eric Habisch

Dr. Fred Bunnell
BY ANTHEA FARR (WIFE OF FRED BUNNELL)

The positive influence that Fred had on the LFN in the 1980s cannot be overestimated. A professor of wildlife ecology in UBC's Forestry Faculty, Fred brought a wealth of knowledge and enthusiasm to the club.

In that decade, LFN membership soared from about 30 to nearly 100 individuals, due in part to the slide-illustrated monthly meeting programs about wildlife, presented by Fred or by his students. Fred wanted to encourage his graduate students to learn how to engage with the public. So much so, that giving talks to the public became a mandatory part of their course work. As a result, our club learned about the students' research on many species of BC wildlife, including Stone Sheep and White Pelicans.

Perhaps the most memorable of all of these wildlife programs was Fred's talk about grizzly bears. A packed audience listened

Fred Bunnell with LFN-planted tree at Forslunds. Photo: Anthea Farr

From left to right: Bob Puls, Glenn Ryder, Al Grass, Jude Grass and Fred Bunnell. Photo: Anne Gosse

to tales about bears—who knew that Fred had two grizzlies on UBC's campus in enclosures that were not, initially, bear-proof? (After contributing to research about bear nutrition, these orphaned bears spent a long and happy retirement at the Kamloops Wildlife Park.) And no, they did not escape at UBC. Fortunately, Fred found out (just in time) what young grizzlies could do to metal when they become strong enough and bored enough.

Many other fascinating research findings about grizzlies were revealed and a great many questions followed. For years afterwards, Fred's bear talk was remembered as one of the best of all LFN programs.

As well as giving talks, Fred also got involved in club projects, such as the Forslund-Watson Wildlife Area (aka "Forslunds") and Brydon Lagoon. Fred's expertise at writing grant proposals came in very handy and with his help, we applied for and received a grant from PCAF (Public Conservation Assistance Fund) to cover costs of work at Forslunds. Our proposal to establish Brydon Lagoon as a nature park, submitted to the City of Langley, was largely successful because of Fred's input into that proposal.

One day, thanks to Fred, our club got some international attention. In 1984, there was an international conference on forestry in Vancouver. Forestry professionals from all over the world attended, including some from Europe. Where better to take them to see *forest management for wildlife* than Forslunds? Fred organized the field trip; a large chartered bus brought attendees to the west side of the property.

There they were met by several LFNers, who proudly took them down the trails to show how we were managing the forest to benefit wildlife. Points of interest on the tour included clearings we had made (by logging patches of the alder-dominated forest), plantings of different kinds of conifer and deciduous trees, wrapping of wire mesh around young tree stems to protect them from deer damage, building of brush piles to provide cover for wildlife, erection of nest boxes and snag creation. The foresters seemed duly impressed, perhaps taking some ideas (such as what volunteers can do) back to their home countries.

Naturally, Fred's students also got involved in LFN projects. At Forslunds, several students recorded birds and other wildlife and then produced reports as part of their course work, undergraduate honours thesis or summer job. Other students were involved with the Fraser Islands Ecological Reserve (another LFN project), measuring trees in plots, and assessing current and potential beaver impacts.

Clearly, in his role as an LFN member, Fred has had a far-ranging impact. How far the "ripples" he created have gone, we may never know.

Anthea Farr BY PHIL HENDERSON

If someone were to ask me, "What is a Langley Field Naturalist?", I would simply point to Anthea. Anthea is the quintessential Langley Field Naturalist. She has all the qualities of a great naturalist: curiosity, patience, observational acuity, focus, and humility. Her involvement with the club since 1980 has been critical to its survival and helped ensure its existence during tough times.

Through her long-term involvement in and commitment to Nature BC's Young Naturalists program as Co-Leader of NatureKids Nicomekl, Anthea has inspired countless youth to understand, appreciate and respect the natural world around them. In this way she has helped each child to develop their own, unique understanding of nature, a blueprint for their naturalist persona and hope for the future of the natural world.

Anthea investigating pond life at Mountain View. Photo: LFN Archives

In 2015, BC Nature presented Anthea with a BC Nature Regional award citing her then 35-year involvement with BC Nature (42 now!), her work with youth as well as her local conservation work, including Forslund-Watson, Brydon Lagoon and Firehall Lake (Brookswood Pond) which, without her involvement, may well have been lost.

In the field Anthea is the quiet one, never far away but always on the prowl, often on the fringes of the group, rooting out things of interest and pointing them out to those near her. Naturalist's tip: always keep an eye on Anthea's whereabouts and stay close. She has developed a keen interest in and knowledge of invertebrates and in particular the pollinators, which she is often in pursuit of with her son, Corey, who shares that passion.

With the LFN, Anthea has had two stints as Newsletter Editor, one as President, and for a long time has taken a leading role in the development and implementation of programs for youth. She has been a key contributor to LFN's biodiversity studies, including Forslund-Watson, Hope Redwoods, Mountain View, and Milaster, to which she has contributed important biological data, management recommendations, expertise, and a critical and disciplined eye to the reports, which she also lends to each edition of LFN's quarterly newsletter.

Anthea Farr in Campbell Valley Park.
Photo: Corey Bunnell

Anthea has contributed to many important academic studies and publications relating to how to reduce the impact we humans have on the natural world here in BC. These have included studies on Bald Eagles, shorebirds, species at-risk, biodiversity, and climate change, for the Government of BC, University of British Columbia, Canadian Wildlife Service, and the World Wildlife Fund.

Anthea's writing and communication skills draw upon pragmatism, humour and creativity. She has a way of describing things that captures one's imagination and educates. I can perhaps sum this up best by proclaiming that Anthea forever altered my notion of the majestic and graceful Great Blue Heron when she pointed out the transformation of a statuesque creek-side bird to a squawking, ungainly "prehistoric creature" when it took flight. My romantic view of this bird was partially and permanently replaced by a more realistic view of a horrifying, merciless predator.

Anthea is a quiet but indomitable force for nature.

ANTHEA'S TIP
Helping butterflies or other pollinators can be as simple as letting some clover bloom in your yard (or in a pot on your patio).

Clouded Sulphur butterfly on Red Clover. Photo: Eric Habisch

Rhys and Annabel Griffiths
BY BOB PULS & ANTHEA FARR

How lucky we were to have this couple join our club! Originally from England and Ireland, Rhys and Annabel joined in 1997,
when the club was truly in the doldrums. At that time, all club
members were given director positions: Rhys was made president,
treasurer and membership director. Annabel became secretary,
a position she held until 2010.

Both of them brought a friendly demeanour and a wealth of
good will and humour. They also brought experience in being
effective as a naturalist (Annabel) or as an environmentalist
(Rhys). Able to connect with others with ease, they helped the
club to grow and to thrive.

Rhys also served as a director to BC Nature (then called Federation of BC Naturalists) and spent two terms as director to the
Langley Environmental Partners Society (LEPS).

Rhys Griffiths scattering grain for the ducks.
Photo: John Gordon (Courtesy Langley Advance Times archives)

Annabel Griffiths (left) with Al Grass (right) in 2014. Photo: Anne Gosse

The goals of LEPS, *protecting and restoring the environment through education, cooperation and action,* fit well with Rhys' environmental philosophy.

As the Griffiths lived in a house overlooking Brydon Lagoon, they soon became the LFN's eyes, ears and guardians of the lagoon. Rhys had no hesitation in visiting the mayor's office if anything needed to be done. Always the gentleman, he expressed his views in such a dignified, friendly and compelling manner that he usually got whatever results were desired.

Vacating the LFN presidency by no means ended Rhys' club activities. He and Annabel initiated a program to control Purple Loosestrife—a serious threat in the Brydon Lagoon area and other Langley area sites. When UBC expertise and equipment was no longer available for this project, Rhys found funding to buy the club's own equipment. He also persuaded Langley City to test the water quality of the lagoon and to install and upgrade an aeration system.

In addition, Rhys spent untold hours working on behalf of the Forslund-Watson Wildlife Area, the property which the LFN manage for the province. He also worked in the Jackman Wetland Park in Aldergrove and participated in the Nicomekl River clean-up every year. A great spokesman for the club, Rhys made sure the LFN was represented at Campbell Valley Country Celebrations and at Rivers Day. He also never failed to carry the club banner in community parades!

Annabel, as well as being LFN secretary for 13 years, was our BC Nature representative from 2008 to 2012. She also served on the Langley in Action Committee, speaking on water and air quality issues. An enthusiastic bird watcher, Annabel participated regularly in the club's Christmas Bird counts and monthly field trips. Any field trip around Brydon Lagoon would usually end up on the Griffiths' back porch, where participants could enjoy the lovely view, a cup of coffee and Annabel's special home-made Irish cookies.

Rhys passed away in 2018 but will never be forgotten by those who knew him. At the lagoon, a commemorative plaque on a rock and three specially planted trees honour Rhys and his legacy. Annabel eventually moved to a retirement home. In 2022, she celebrated her 90th birthday at a horse farm owned by friends in Abbotsford, an event eagerly attended by many LFN members. And of course, she still retains her passion for birds!

Both Rhys and Annabel received honours and awards for their service to the Langley Field Naturalists, BC Nature, LEPS, Langley City and Langley Township. In 2012, Rhys was also awarded the Queen's Diamond Jubilee Medal.

Dr. Martin McNicholl
BY ANTHEA FARR &
PHIL HENDERSON

Dr. Martin McNicholl.
Photo: LFN Archives

A passion for birds is one of the gifts that Dr. Martin McNicholl brought to the LFN. This passion developed at a very early age. Born and raised in Winnipeg, Martin said that his first memory of a bird, at age three, was a Common Loon yodeling as it flew over a rowboat containing him, his father, and his grandfather.

As a university student, Martin studied waterbirds, Sharp-tailed Grouse, Forster's Terns, and Blue Grouse (now called Sooty Grouse). His professional life included managing and directing Long Point Bird Observatory in Ontario, conducting many ornithological field programs, and working on reducing bird strikes at Vancouver International Airport.

Martin's enthusiasm for birds manifested itself in our club in several ways. For many years, he organized our section of the Christmas Bird Count, as well as participating in it himself. Snow, rain, wind, fog or cold, no matter, Martin would be out there with the rest of us, counting birds. At the post-count gatherings, his knowledge of birds was an asset, as there could sometimes be questionable species to discuss.

And who could forget Martin's almost impossible bird quizzes at LFN meetings? He would project a photo of part of a bird, maybe just its foot or its beak. Or there might be an entire bird, but it would be partially obscured by vegetation, as is often the case in the real world. These quizzes would elicit groans as well as smiles. One thing was certain—once exposed to such a quiz, most naturalists in the room realized they still had much to learn about bird identification!

Martin was also our program convener for many years. Making use of his many contacts with other scientists, Martin ensured that there was no shortage of educational and enlightening programs at our general meetings. Often, he had a personal connection with the speaker and would add amusing anecdotes when he introduced him or her. During the talk, Martin kept notes and later wrote a summary of the salient points. This was submitted to the LFN newsletter editor, providing a useful reference for both attendees and for those who had missed the talk.

Having spent time in Cuba working as an ornithologist, Martin presented his own program on Cuban birdlife one evening at an LFN meeting. How envious we became as we gawked at his photos of the fabulous and colourful Cuban birds—new and

---

Some of the awards given to Martin include the following:

- the **Loran L. Goulden Award** for contributions to the natural history of Alberta (1983)

- the **Ernest Thompson Seton medal** for contributions to Manitoba's natural history (1995) and

- the **Steve Cannings Award** for contributions to ornithology in BC (2014).

Martin socializing with Nanny Mulder ten Kate. Photo: LFN Archives

exotic to almost all of us. I think many of us developed a sudden desire to visit that country.

Even after a bout of meningitis which resulted in a lengthy coma and left him with permanent side effects, Martin rallied and inspired us all, as he "kept on going." During his long hospital stay, he compiled a list of all the birds he saw through his hospital window.

Although he was no longer able to do field work in the years that followed, he continued to write, edit and review publications about birds and to find little-known scientific papers for other ornithologists. As always, he found time to spend with naturalists such as those in the LFN. He took great pleasure in encouraging us, and others, to appreciate the natural world.

Phil Henderson
BY ANTHEA FARR

Were it not for Phil Henderson, none of us would have noticed, let alone been introduced to, the liverwort nicknamed after a cartoon mouse. Small, green, damp, this one stands out. Like all leafy liverworts, it has "leaves" (technically they are leaf-like structures) arranged in two or three

Phil Henderson
Photo: Elly McNeilly

rows in a flattened pattern. But the "leaves" on this species are divided into threes, like the three-fingered hands of a very famous cartoon mouse. The nickname Phil gave it is much easier to remember than *Lepidozia reptans*. (Another common name is the "Little Hands" liverwort).

Phil knows his mosses and he knows his liverworts, rather rare qualities in the naturalist community. We are honoured to have a

Little Hands Liverwort.
Photo: Shona Ellis

member who can introduce us to the unknown and secret natural world of the "very tiny". Thanks to Phil, we have also met the "electrified cat's tail moss" (*Rhytidiadelphus triquetrus*), a plant that looks like it just had a violent electric shock. And so many more. One could spend an hour just looking at one tree trunk…

Yet Phil is actually an all-round

naturalist, as was his friend and long-time mentor, Glenn Ryder. Phil learned from one of the very best. He is also a professional biologist, working all over western Canada on different contracts. In his spare time, Phil organizes, takes part in, and summarizes the Fort Langley Bird Count each February, takes part in the LFN section of the Christmas Bird Count each year and leads LFN field trips. He also helps with plant inventories or whatever else is needed on various LFN projects.

His writing and editing skills are excellent; for many years he was the editor of the LFN newsletter. We appreciate all that Phil has done for the club, but we also admire his modesty, friendly demeanour and his unique sense of humour. Finally, we applaud his efforts to help naturalists learn about the "small, green and tiny", often an uphill battle when there are brightly-coloured birds flying about!

Left: Phil Henderson at Milaster. Photo: Anthea Farr
Right: Hanging moss coated with frost. Photo: Bob Puls

Roy Yates
BY BOB PULS &
PHIL HENDERSON

Roy Yates at Forslund-Watson.
Photo: Anthea Farr

Roy Yates joined the LFN in 1998, having previously belonged to the Vancouver Natural History Society. He started volunteering as a Campbell Valley Park Nature House host in 2002. Roy avoided club politics and never served on the LFN board but was always a willing project helper. Among the many projects he helped with were Brydon Lagoon maintenance, Mountain View Crown Land trail blazing, Forslund-Watson upkeep, the LFN Raptor Count, and Great Horned Owl nest monitoring. Roy also remembers helping distribute beetles for the Purple Loosestrife project, particularly the day when he "sucked instead of blew and got a mouth full of beetles"—no harm done, and he survived.

Roy was also an eager participant in a bird banding trial at the Forslund-Watson Wildlife Area, led by Derek and Carol Matthews of the Vancouver Avian Research Centre. At that time, Derek and Carol were looking to establish a banding station and chose Forslund-Watson as a potential site, before finally settling on their current location at Colony Farm. Roy was key in facilitating the trials, helping to set up the station on those early weekend mornings and keen to learn all he could about the process and the birds caught in the mist nets. Eager to continue learning about the birds after this introduction to banding, he enrolled in and completed Cornell's Comprehensive Bird Biology course.

He has regularly attended LFN's monthly meetings and joined various field trips. Conversations with Roy are always interesting, whether the topic is birds, sailing, mountaineering or something completely different. Roy is knowledgeable, quiet, and unassuming—great attributes of a field naturalist.

Anthea Farr, Bob Puls and Roy Yates trail blazing at Mountain View Crown Lands. On this hike, Anthea said "Don't you dare cut down those bent Vine Maples—they are covered in hanging moss!" We diverted around them. Photo: Al Grass

Robert (Bob) Puls
BY SHEILA PULS & ANTHEA FARR

Bob is a "born naturalist", raised in the countryside of Monmouthshire in South Wales. Many of his teenage years were spent birdwatching and controlling Wood Pigeons and rabbits in the surrounding farmland. His first bio-inventory was a survey of the flora of a patch of woodland for his A-level Botany thesis, for which he used an ancient Argus 35mm camera that his father passed on to him to record the plants. Subsequently he purchased his own camera and photography replaced the shotgun.

After graduating from Agricultural College, he emigrated to Canada and eventually moved to BC in 1969, where he worked for 35 years with the Veterinary Branch of the Ministry of Agriculture. After Bob retired, it was not too hard for Rhys Griffiths to twist his arm into joining the Langley Field Naturalists, and to later cajole him into taking on the President's position. Bob served as President for a record ten years, before happily passing it on to Lisa Dreves.

Bob Puls in 2016, camera at the ready. Photo: LFN Archives

He continues to act as Conservation Chair, a position rife with frustrating challenges and welcome opportunities. Those welcome opportunities included bio-inventories of Hope Redwoods Natural Area, Mountain View Crown Lands and Milaster Passive Park. Bob has also enjoyed leading and participating in field trips and taking part in the BC Nature spring and fall meetings, always *enjoying nature and trying to keep it worth knowing.*

He and his wife live on a small sheep farm in south Aldergrove. During lambing season, Bob and Sheila host LFN executive meetings at their home so that they can keep an eye on their ewes. These meetings are eagerly attended by LFN members who love to watch both frolicking lambs and the variety of common and rare birds that flock to the Puls' well-stocked bird feeders.

Sheila Puls
BY LILIANNE FULLER

Sheila Puls describes herself as an SOB or a Spouse of Birder! Sheila was born in Chichester, England, where she has many memories of family picnics in the countryside, picking bluebells and primroses in the local woods. This was where her first love of nature was kindled.

Sheila and Bob Puls.
Photo: Elly McNeilly

The family moved several times due to her father's work as a municipal engineer. This must have given her a love of moving, because after training as a secretary/office administrator, she hit the road for a "Have typewriter–Will travel" trip to see the world.

She arrived in Ontario in 1968 and, after exploring Eastern Canada, she set out for Vancouver. From Vancouver, she planned her ongoing journey to the Orient and then on to New Zealand. But fate had other plans and she met husband-to-be, Bob Puls, who decided to buy her a ticket back to Vancouver from New Zealand. Settling in Aldergrove, she and Bob enjoyed a rural lifestyle, raising and preserving much of their own food. Over the years, they raised sheep, chickens, turkeys and rabbits and grew a variety of fruit and vegetables. They also raised two sons and various cats and dogs!

They joined LFN when Bob retired. A few years later, Sheila took on the job of Newsletter Editor and subsequently added Membership to her responsibilities. She also undertook the big job of co-coordinating the 2010 BC Nature Fall Meeting with Jude Grass and then the 2023 BC Nature AGM & Conference. Sheila also serves as a director of BC Nature and the BC Naturalists' Foundation.

Although she loves nature, Sheila is still not an expert, but has many happy memories of time spent with other members. These include hosting meetings in her home, enjoying the BC Nature annual and fall meetings in other parts of the province, and driving experts around on bird counts or compiling their data afterwards.

For many years of the Fort Langley Bird Count, before the days of eBird, Sheila efficiently and without complaint compiled data on her laptop for each of the six routes as weather-weary and bedraggled participants returned with their soggy field sheets. Sheila made sure the church basement was warm and inviting with fresh coffee, assorted teas and treats, kind words and a smile.

What else to say? Let us raise our wine glasses in a toast to this dedicated LFN couple!

CHAPTER 3

Forslund-Watson: Land for Wildlife

by Anthea Farr & Bob Puls

> "The land was good to us and in the early pioneering days the wildlife helped us survive. This is a way of saying thanks..."– **ALBERT FORSLUND**

Beginnings

Albert's bright eyes remind me of a spring morning, full of promise. The "promise" is to regale me, or any of the other naturalists who visit him, with tales of his boyhood. He will take us back to the early 1900s, to a simpler and wilder Langley. We, the listeners, soon have little doubt that Albert and his three brothers (Walter, William and James) were clever and resourceful boys. They were also adept at hunting. The wildlife, including deer, elk, bear, lynx and bobcat, was either eaten, sold as pelts or cashed in for bounty, all of which helped keep the family alive.

Albert can't resist telling us about his successful hunt of a large tom bobcat. The cat had been cornered by the family's two dogs. Not willing to use his last rifle shell, Albert instead pulled out his pocket knife and cut a long pole of vine maple. It just took one hard knock on the cat's head to end the hunt. The reward was a bounty of $1.25, the going price for a cat.

Bees were another kind of wildlife that helped the family survive. Flying around in the Forslunds' woods were European Honey Bees (that may have flown across the border from Washington). "We found their hives," Albert says proudly. "Do you know how? We sprinkled flour on the bees in different locations, then mapped

Facing: A summer evening LFN field trip on the property. The Wildlife Area is not open to the public and has a live-in caretaker. Those wishing to visit are welcome to come on an LFN-guided walk. Photo: Anthea Farr

Albert Forslund. Photo: Anthea Farr

which direction they flew. Then we used triangulation to figure out the location of the hive." The first hive they found was in 1913. It yielded 100 pounds of honey, which could be sold for about 33 dollars.

As well as being resourceful, I think the boys also had a wild streak—wilder than most. Albert leans forward and tells me with a smile: "We blew up a big tree with dynamite!" He then elaborates how he did that. Although I don't remember the "why", I am sure there was a practical reason. I do know that some forest had to be cleared to make room for pasture.

Cows need a lot of grass. Their father, John Forslund, had decided to become a dairy farmer. Born in Sweden, John left his homeland in 1876 to come to North America. After landing in New York, he worked in logging camps in the U.S., then moved to Canada to work on the Canadian Pacific Railway. In 1886, he settled in south Langley, homesteading a property where huge cedars and firs grew. Some of this forest had to be logged to bring his farming dream to fruition. When his new roots were firmly in place, John married Mary Eliza Carlson, who bore him one daughter, Ethel, and four sons: Walter, Albert, William, and James.

For Posterity

In 1975, Albert and his brother Walter, their niece Shirley Watson and her husband, Bruce Watson, donated a total of 58 acres (23.5 hectares) to the BC Land Commission, to be kept in perpetuity as a gift for wildlife. Environmentalists and naturalists across the Lower Mainland were delighted; some came to visit and chat with Albert.

"We didn't want to have it destroyed... we kept it so long and we wouldn't let nobody go in and cut wood or nothing else, so come to our age and we're wildlife lovers here... so we decided to donate (our property) to the Land Commission..."—**ALBERT FORSLUND**

Visiting aside, the naturalists still had an issue to resolve. Although the Land Commission had acquired ownership, it had no mandate or staff to manage the property. Eagerly, the LFN stepped into this void. After years of meetings, in 1980 the LFN Society finally obtained written permission to manage the property. Now there was an opportunity to stop unwanted intrusions and better protect the land, as well as making some changes to increase wildlife diversity.

"He (Albert) was born on that homestead... and it was soon apparent that every other living thing there shared it with him—the deer that came to the house, the swallows that nested against the house walls, the hummingbirds that fed at feeders outside the window and various other birds at well-stocked feeders and the trees growing in the wooded area."

— **MARGARET LANGFORD,**
WHITE ROCK AND SURREY NATURALIST

Full Speed Ahead

HOW TO PROTECT THE LAND?

When the LFN became managers of this land, neighbours were riding their horses and children were riding their mini-bikes all over it. The LFN executive came up with two action plans:

1) build and maintain fences and post "No Trespassing" signs, and

2) canvas the neighbours to provide them with information and to assess their respect for the area.

In due time these tasks were completed and deemed successful.

Forslund heritage apple tree.
Photo: Bob Puls

HOW TO INCREASE WILDLIFE DIVERSITY?

Although the gift encompassed woods, fields and ephemeral wetlands, those woods in 1980 consisted mainly of an even-aged stand of 40-year-old alders. Not the most diverse forest! But how diverse? An inventory was needed to discover just what else was there.

Members began an inventory in the spring of 1981 and completed it in November of that year. John Ellens documented all the plants he found and other members recorded the fauna, mostly birds. Once that was done, LFN member Natalie Minunzie felt the club should apply for government funds: the Habitat Conservation Fund and the Public Conservation Assistance Fund. These applications were successful and the funds provided salary for a senior UBC student, Dave Dunbar, to create a long-term management plan for the area. The funds also covered other costs, such as purchase of seedlings, a chain saw and a ladder, and the hiring of a contractor to deepen the ponds. The LFN were going "full speed ahead."

LFN member Natalie Minunzie at a tree planting bee at Forslunds. Natalie played a key role as the early liaison between Albert Forslund, the LFN and the BC Land Commission to establish the reserve.
Photo: Anthea Farr

Planting bee in a new clearing in the 1980s. Photo: LFN Archives

Dave Dunbar's plan called for many actions, such as creating clearings in the forest, planting conifers and fruit-bearing trees and shrubs, creating snags, putting up nest boxes, creating hedgerows, controlling blackberry, and deepening a pond. The club's chain saw, as well as a few personal chain saws, came in handy for the first task of creating clearings. We were fortunate, too, that some LFN members had logging experience.

Once toppled, the trees' limbs were removed, bucked and stacked to build brush piles. Members not wielding saws placed smaller branches on the tops of the brush piles. The resulting piles, nicknamed "twigloos", would provide cover for wildlife. Almost instantly, the twigloos were adopted by Bewick's Wrens and Song Sparrows.

Next, there was planting to be done. A lot of planting. Three hundred and twenty-one broadleaf trees and shrubs and

90 conifer seedlings were awaiting a new home. To help achieve this, the LFN was joined by seven White Rock and Surrey Naturalists (WR&S), some UBC students and a next-door neighbour, Hart Long. Many hours of digging ensued, with the last of these trees placed in the ground in April, 1983.

Also, on the "to-do" list was training for LFN and WR&S naturalists to conduct more scientifically robust bird surveys. Four transect lines with bird listening stations were created and participants learned the Unlimited Distance Point Count Method. For several years, monthly counts were conducted, especially during the breeding season. The results showed that stations in the newly-created clearings had more species and more individuals of birds than stations in dense woods. All of our sweat and labour were paying off.

But changes were coming, and the LFN would have to adapt. By 1985, the Land Commission had decided to get out of land ownership. That year, Albert was so pleased with what the LFN had achieved that he donated another 19 acres (7.7 hectares) and suggested that the club take on land ownership. But the LFN executive had valid concerns, not the least of which was the possibility that our small club could fold.

The BC Ministry of Environment (currently, BC Ministry of Land, Water and Resource Stewardship) seemed a better and more secure fit and it has remained the owner of this "Wildlife Area" to date. Another change came in 1990 when the LFN was unable to pay for liability insurance premiums then required by the Ministry. The solution was to have the Wild Bird Trust as our co-manager, an arrangement which lasted several years, benefitting both Societies, until it was no longer needed.

Some Like It Wet

Most months of the year, gumboots are a necessity to keep one's feet dry anywhere on the property. But, as noted previously, in the early years all the wetlands and ponds were ephemeral, drying up in late summer or fall. Dave Dunbar's management recommendation to deepen a pond addressed this issue and would ensure water was available to wildlife year-round. And so, in the 1980s, the pond project began. Little did we know at that time, that one pond would lead to another, and another, and another.

The first of these was already in place, in the woods, and had been built by the Forslunds to provide a watering hole for their cattle. A bit of deepening was needed to help it retain water longer and years later it became known as the LFN Pond. The second pond project was the largest and most ambitious, located in the northeast corner of the property. Funded by grant money and built by Ducks Unlimited (DU), it had a proper water control structure and small dam. For decades, this pond was called the "Permanent Pond"—until it dried up during the heat dome of 2021. Now known as the DU Pond, it has hosted large numbers of waterfowl in fall, winter and spring, with an occasional pair remaining to breed in summer.

The third pond, built in a naturally wet depression in the hay field, was initially called the "Vernal Pond." This name was changed to "Bob's Pond" when the fourth and fifth ponds, also vernal, were built in 2021 and 2022 by BCIT (British Columbia Institute of Technology). Located in another naturally wet depression, in the upper hay field, these "last" two ponds are referred to as the BCIT Ponds.

These sources of fresh water host aquatic or semi-aquatic plants and attract many creatures, including mammals such as deer,

Top: First BCIT pond, September 2021. Photo: Bob Puls
Bottom Left: Pacific Chorus Frog. Photo: Corey Bunnell
Bottom Right: Variegated Meadowhawk Dragonfly. Photo: Eric Habisch

coyotes, raccoons, and even the occasional muskrat or bobcat. The ponds have also contributed to the property's growing list of birds, which is now at 145 species and includes 21 species of waterfowl (ducks, geese and swans). Pacific Chorus Frogs and Northwestern Salamanders are some of the amphibians that breed in two or three of our ponds each year. At least 27 species of dragonflies have been recorded and many native plants, including sedges, rushes, and bryophytes, have colonized pond edges.

A Chance To Learn

Students and their professors have long been involved with this property, contributing labour, ideas or even potted plants, from institutions such as UBC, SFU, Pearson College, Trinity Western and BCIT. Although not all ideas were deemed equal, many enhanced wildlife habitat and had either a short-term or long-term positive benefit. Best of all, it was an opportunity for environmental students to learn practical and useful skills, with naturalists learning with them.

The young people whom the LFN got to know best came to Langley in 1984. "Katimavik", an Inuit word which means "meeting place", was a federal make-work program for young Canadians aged 17 to 21. In return for free labour, the LFN members were required to billet these "kids": provide room and board, ferry them to and from the work site (Forslunds), and provide some supervision. Although they were coming from Quebec and other parts of eastern Canada, we could specify that they should know English, as well as French. This was fortunate.

Nearly all of the LFN executive members participated. After a week of billeting, we felt we knew these young folks quite well. Safety concerns were less stringent back then; the kids were all given hard hats and machetes. The machetes were long and sharp.

Thankfully, there were no injuries while the kids learned how to wield machetes effectively. Much was accomplished. Three new clearings were enhanced with well-built brush piles, trails were cleared and nearly 3,000 conifer seedlings were planted— mostly where we wanted them to be.

Changes

Change is inevitable, and over the past five decades, the LFN has observed various changes to the property and its inhabitants. Some of these changes mirror much more widespread changes that have occurred across the Lower Mainland, or even across North America. Birds that we saw there in the 80s and 90s that are now rare—or gone—include Olive-sided Flycatcher, Band-tailed Pigeon, Evening Grosbeak, Ruffed Grouse, and Western Screech-Owl. Newcomers, now common, include Anna's Hummingbird, Barred Owl, and Eurasian Collared-Dove.

Mammals and amphibians too have changed: Flying Squirrels no longer poke their heads out of our nest boxes and Red-legged Frogs and Rough-skinned Newts have not been seen there for years.

Left: Rough-skinned Newt. This species has a neurotoxin in its skin which deters most predators, but some garter snakes are immune. Photo: Wim Vesseur
Right: The Western Screech-Owl population has declined due to habitat loss and the invasion of Barred Owls. Photo: John Gordon

Albert Forslund, who had been made an honorary member of both the Langley Field Naturalists and the White Rock & Surrey Naturalists, died in 1992 at the age of 92. Descendants of the deer that helped his family survive still roam forest and field and leave tracks by the ponds where they come to drink. So too did a bobcat, which would have really pleased Albert.

The Forslunds' historic barn with its hand-hewn timbers succumbed to a wind storm in December, 1998. Sadly, the resident pair of Barn Owls then had to search for a new home. Efforts to diversify the forest continued. Our LFN Conservation Chair, Bob Puls, raised 150 Western Redcedars in pots, which were planted in the forest from 2009 to 2011. Some of these trees have now reached a height of 20 feet (about 6 meters). Below the canopy, spring wildflowers still delight: trillium, bleeding heart, miner's lettuce, fringecup, false lily-of-the-valley, skunk cabbage.

LFN member Ryan Usenik, our present liaison with the Ministry, has been busy this past decade. As well as the usual tasks involving fences, gates, invasive species control, trail maintenance, organizing hay mowing and writing reports, he organized bat

YELLOW ARCHANGEL

Yellow Archangel *(Lamium galeobdolon)* is one of the invasive species found in the reserve. LFN members, especially Jenny and Ben Auxier, and LEPS crews spent countless hours pulling up this plant to curtail and reduce its spread in the reserve's forest.

Photo: Bob Puls

surveys. Who knew the Mexican Free-tailed was one of the bat species feeding above the DU Pond in summer? At the edge of the hay field, Ryan also installed a bat box and a Barn Owl box. No takers yet, but they provide popular perching sites for swallows and sparrows. A Wood Duck box Ryan put up at Bob's Pond has been happily used by Hooded Mergansers, while another one attached below a bat box near the DU Pond has been gratefully accepted by a pair of American Kestrels.

Bob Puls has also been busy in the nest box department, installing four Wood Duck boxes at the DU Pond in 2011 and 2012. These were successfully used by Wood Ducks. He also installed many swallow boxes along the north edge of the hay field. These have been used by Tree Swallows, Violet-green Swallows, Deer Mice and House Wrens (the latter having migrated north to establish its territory here in 2017).

Both Ryan and Bob make sure surveys continue: amphibians, birds, and dragonflies. We have been fortunate to have had two young Langley birders, Viktor and Marnix Vandereyk, take on the bird surveys for us—both are graduates of Melissa Hafting's Young Birders Program in Vancouver. They are "hot shot" birders and we appreciate them immensely.

From the hay field, we watch the Red-tailed Hawks soar above us, sending harsh calls if they think we are too close to their nest tree. At our feet, small spiders scuttle in the grass while a nearby Savannah Sparrow keeps a watchful eye. Deep in the forest, Great Horned Owls are still nesting, raising healthy broods of owlets.

These things have not changed in the past 50 years. We know there will be changes and new challenges ahead. For now, all is well. We are honouring Albert's wishes, keeping this a place for wildlife.

CHAPTER 4

Brydon Lagoon: The Jewel of Langley City

by Anthea Farr & Bob Puls

"We arrived at Brydon Lagoon with several logs on a trailer, which we had collected from a couple of donor sites. These were to replace older floating roosts that had become water-logged and were starting to sink. We slid the first log into the water, but it stuck in the mud. What to do? Someone had to lift the end so it would slide further into the pond and float. Off came my boots and socks and into the murky water I waded. I lifted the log so it could slide out farther. The other logs soon followed, but what was the feeling that something was nibbling on my toes? I hoped there were no large snapping turtles in there! Several years later when a large fish kill occurred, we were amazed at how many little toe-nibbling species were in the lagoon."

— **BOB PULS**

Beginnings

Brydon Lagoon had humble beginnings as a sewage lagoon for the City of Langley. It was named after the Brydon family who homesteaded the area in the early 1900s. But the region's history goes back much further than that.

The Nicomekl River that flows through this area was used by local First Nations as part of their travelling route between Fort Langley and their relatives to the south, in what is now the United States. They would portage their canoes between the Nicomekl

Facing: Brydon Lagoon. Photo: Anthea Farr

and Salmon Rivers (the same route that the Hudson's Bay Company travelled on their way to explore the Fraser River in 1826). The word *Nicomekl* comes from the Halq'emeylem language, a Central Salish language of the Pacific Northwest, meaning "the route to go" or "the pathway." In about 1910, the British Columbia Electric Company built their Interurban railway line through the property, and it is their right-of-way that parallels the southern shore of Brydon Lagoon. Exactly 100 feet (30.5 meters) above sea level, this right-of-way has been used by cyclists, joggers and walkers of all ages.

In 1955, the City of Langley separated from the Township of Langley after a dispute concerning the provision of streetlights. By 1961, the City's need for a sanitary sewer system had become increasingly important. A decision was made to build a sewage lagoon on the west side of the city, at 198th Street and 53rd Avenue near the Nicomekl River floodplain.

For 12 years, from 1963 until 1975, this lagoon functioned as a primary sewage treatment facility. It removed much of the waste that had previously flowed directly into the Nicomekl River, either via sanitary or storm sewer. Although it was close to the river, the lagoon was never breached by high water until after it was decommissioned. In 1975, it was no longer needed as the City then connected to GVRD's sewer system. Brydon Lagoon was left to evolve naturally into a refuge for waterfowl and other wildlife.

Enter The Langley Field Naturalists (LFN)

The Langley Field Naturalists started to take an interest in the lagoon site soon after the GVRD sewer trunk line was completed. Bird counts in the area indicated large numbers. At this time Anthea Farr was president of the Langley Field Naturalists and

First planting bee at Brydon Lagoon. Photo: LFN Archives

wanted to see the LFN save the area as a nature park. To that end, she submitted a detailed proposal to Langley City dated August 31st, 1984: *A Proposal to Enhance the Value of the former Langley Sewage Lagoon.*

There were other ideas presented to the City, such as filling it in and establishing a trailer park or turning it into a remote-controlled boat site, but the city favoured the LFN plan and in 1985 designated Brydon Lagoon and the adjacent 2.5 acres (1 hectare) of forest to the north as a Nature Reserve. Thus began LFN's good working relationship with the City of Langley, one that has lasted decades.

Brydon Lagoon is Transformed

The club obtained funding from the Public Conservation Assistance Fund to help their cause. Members then put in hundreds of hours enhancing the area for both human and avian visitors. The tasks undertaken by these members were varied and required a surprisingly wide range of skills.

Bushes and trees to attract more songbirds were purchased and planted by members with good, strong backs. Some of these same members pushed wheelbarrows of hog fuel to create rough trails around the lagoon. With help from Ducks Unlimited (DU) staff, LFN members hammered together and launched a floating raft for waterfowl which was quickly adopted by a pair of Canada Geese. Member John Cleghorn used his carpentry skills to build a raised wooden viewing platform that extended out over the water in the southeast corner. Others built nest boxes to be put on top of posts or nailed high up on trees by members without fear of heights.

An informative pamphlet about the lagoon was published by the LFN and handed out to the public by members with good social skills. Lagoon signs were designed and posted to enlighten

Getting ready to launch a raft for waterfowl. From left to right: Irene Pearce, Fred Bunnell, Kathleen Fry, Herb Pastrick. Photo: LFN Archives

Left: Feeding ducks at Brydon. Photo: John Gordon
Right: Brydon dog signage. Photo: Bob Puls

visitors, including one entitled "Healthy Food – Healthy Ducks", which encouraged visitors to feed the ducks grains and seeds rather than bread. Club members Mary Pastrick and Irene Pearce gave guided nature walks around the lagoon for students from the nearby Nicomekl Elementary School. They also supervised other activities for the students, such as painting yellow fish symbols beside storm drains north of the lagoon.

Brydon Lagoon is Maintained

There are several tasks that the LFN, the City, or LEPS (Langley Environmental Partners Society) must complete regularly: trees have to be protected from beavers, who find them very enticing; the trails, which were brought up to public access standards by the City of Langley, must be maintained; benches have to be repaired and upgraded; and nest boxes have to be checked each year and re-paired when needed. LEPS, sometimes assisted by LFN, regularly conduct fish surveys, remove blackberry, and plant native shrubs.

The floating raft and wooden viewing platform were well used and lasted several years. LFN replaced the raft with several

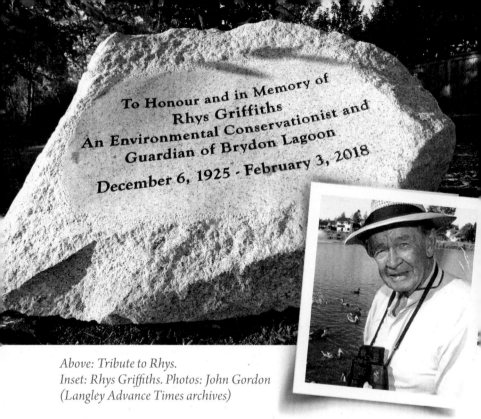

Above: Tribute to Rhys.
Inset: Rhys Griffiths. Photos: John Gordon
(Langley Advance Times archives)

anchored logs, which need re-positioning or replacing when they sink or drift too close to shore. Where the viewing platform used to be, the City built a gravel beach, accessible to all for viewing and feeding ducks. But wherever people go, garbage follows; collecting litter is ongoing by the City, LEPS, LFN and caring neighbours.

LFN has been fortunate to have had members as "guardians". The first one was Judy Parkman who lived close to the lagoon and kept the club well informed about the goings-on there. In 1997, Rhys and Annabel Griffiths moved into a house overlooking the lagoon and became passionate stewards and guardians until Rhys passed in 2018. Their presence, and willingness to express their concerns to residents, visitors, Mayor and Council ensured Brydon Lagoon's role and legacy as an important natural feature for conservation and education. In honour of Rhys, a large, inscribed rock sits near the southeast entrance to the lagoon. At present, we are lucky to have LFN members Sandy and Kirby Hanawalt, whose house is "a stone's throw" from the lagoon.

Fish

At no time has the lagoon been officially stocked with fish, but over the years many non-native species have found a home there, some probably released from home aquariums. In addition, fish may have been brought in on flood waters from the nearby Nicomekl River. Recent studies have found that some waterfowl can excrete viable carp eggs, thereby transplanting carp from one pond to another.

A massive fish kill in August of 2014 was attributed to high water temperature (29°C) and low oxygen levels. This wasn't the first time this had happened, but it was by far the most severe. Thousands of fish floated to the surface and quickly decomposed over a hot long weekend.

BRYDON POND

Brydon Pond is the Lagoon's smaller neighbour to the southeast. Located in the Nicomekl River floodplain, it lies north of the river and south of the Lagoon's parking lot. It is fed by Muckle Creek, a small tributary of the Nicomekl River. For years, Brydon Pond was maintained by a dam on its eastern outflow which fed into the Nicomekl. Shorebirds and overwintering ducks enjoyed this less busy, quieter retreat, until the dam was removed and the pond virtually drained. It was restored in 2017 when beavers moved in and re-dammed the outlet.

Left: 2014 Fish Kill. Photo: Anthea Farr
Right: Green Heron fishing. Photo: John Gordon

The stench was overpowering, but the herons didn't seem to mind and happily gorged themselves on as many fish as they could eat. LEPS staff had the delightful job of cleaning up the decomposing mess. Non-native fish corpses included several six-pound Eurasian Carp, as well as thousands of smaller fish, such as catfish, sunfish, and minnows: a multitude of "toe-nibblers". The only native species was the Three-spined Stickleback. Not all fish died; some survived and multiplied.

To prevent a repeat occurrence of the fish kill, aeration fountains were repaired, and an underwater bubbling system was installed. The smelly event also spurred the City of Langley to form a Brydon Lagoon Task Force, a subcommittee of the City Parks Environment and Recreation Committee (PERC). Several LFN members served on this task force and a report with recommendations was submitted to City Council in 2016. Recommendations addressing the safety of ducklings and humans were quickly acted upon; others are still awaiting action. The "bubblers" have worked very well. Even the heat dome of 2021 resulted in no fish kills, thanks to those bubblers keeping oxygen levels high enough for fish to survive.

And now?

LFN continue to monitor birds and other wildlife at Brydon Lagoon. In 2021, 137 bird species had been recorded in the park and the site had become an eBird hot spot. It attracts birders from near and far; even attendees at an international bird conference in Vancouver came. Locals also come to feed ducks or to enjoy the peaceful ambiance of nature. Or maybe—just maybe—they come to watch a drama unfold?

The catfish was almost too big. Its captor, a young merganser, knew it had to be swallowed headfirst, not sideways like it was now. Even then, it would be a challenge. The young merganser dropped the fish back into the water to have another go at positioning it just the right way.

Suddenly an older merganser surfaced abruptly from the depths, right where the fish was. One swift grab with its beak, and the older bird was swimming away at top speed with its stolen prize, soon outracing its pursuer. Then it paused and, with practiced gulps, swallowed the big fish whole.

"Better than watching TV!" gleefully remarked another nature watcher. I smiled and resumed my walk around the lagoon, hoping to see more "nature documentaries" in real time. — **ANTHEA FARR**

CHAPTER 5

Conservation and Stewardship: Keeping it Wild

"Every little bit helps. It's amazing how much you can do when you choose to give a little bit of that natural habitat back."

— ROXANNE PAUL, NATIONAL WILDLIFE FEDERATION

The past 50 years have seen huge changes in Langley, with development accelerating and natural habitat shrinking at an ever-increasing rate. This trend has challenged our club and has certainly kept our conservation committee busy. Bob Puls, LFN Conservation Chair for the last 10 years, put it this way: conservation is probably the most challenging, frustrating, and time-consuming part of *Keeping Nature worth Knowing.*

The LFN started with a conservation battle, and battles have continued, as well as conservation projects undertaken with the blessing of others. LFN prefers these amicable conservation projects; it means others, too, understand the importance of conserving natural areas. When necessary, though, the LFN is always willing to fight for nature and over the years we've "won some and lost some." Some natural areas were saved, and some harmful land uses were halted. We are immensely proud of

Facing: 2014. Using a live trap to see if Northern Red-legged Frog tadpoles exist at the DU Pond at Forslund-Watson. Left to Right: Ryan Usenik, Kirk Miles and daughter Kathryn. Photo: LFN Archives

our successes, usually the result of hard work, perseverance and collaborating with other groups.

Some of these, such as Campbell Valley Regional Park, Forslund-Watson Wildlife Area, and Brydon Lagoon, are described in earlier chapters. In this chapter, we profile a few other conservation projects in Langley that may be less well known: the Municipal Natural Park and the Irene Pearce Trail, Hope Redwoods Natural Area, Mountain View Crown Lands, Milaster Passive Park, and the Beetle Project.

Unless someone like you cares a whole awful lot, nothing is going to get better. It's not.
– The Lorax

Seuss, Dr. The Lorax. Random House, 1971. Graphic used with permission, Random House – Penguin Publishing.

Municipal Natural Park & the Irene Pearce Trail
BY ANTHEA FARR & BOB PULS

The throaty calls of the resident ravens carry through the mist, transporting us back to a time when the Little Campbell River was known to First Nations as *Tatalu*. The river is still wild in places. Beavers, muskrats and mink pass through or linger. We have seen them from the park's western bridge, a place where frogs can rival songbirds with their loud chorus. *Tatalu*. Worth fighting for, worth caring for.

Tranquil now, this land and its future were once hotly contested. Confrontation, hard work and persistence were required for the struggles that lay ahead. Bob Puls describes how the battle ensued:

> *"It's 1991 and the Township of Langley has poked a hornet's nest. Site 19 has been purchased as a potential gravel extraction site, and the locals will have none of it! The Council of Rate Payers, formed by the amalgamation of a number of*

Little Campbell River in the Municipal Natural Park.
Photo: Anthea Farr

Irene Pearce (left) and a friend (right) enjoying nature.
Photo: Anthea Farr

Langley rate-payer groups who opposed gravel extraction,
along with the LFN, are rising to the challenge."

The intense lobbying to save this parcel in its natural state was spearheaded by LFN member Irene Pearce. Soft-spoken but determined, Irene put her schoolteacher demeanour to good use when dealing with the Township of Langley. As well as a naturalist, she was a proud owner of an Arabian horse, so she also brought the equestrian perspective to the table. Here was an opportunity to advance the Community Trails Project for walkers and for riders.

Meetings to plan tactics were held at the home of LFNers George and Gail Wool. Other key LFN members in this battle were Natalie Minunzie and Judy Parkman. A huge benefit was having records of the site's wildlife, provided by Glenn Ryder. Faced with so much opposition from so many, the Township backed down. Victory came when the site was re-zoned as a Municipal Natural Park in 1992.

Located north of 4th Avenue between 224th and 232nd Streets, the park has a variety of habitats, including mature Douglas-fir forests (sprinkled with large cedars and big-leaf maples), riparian shrubbery, and one very special stream: the Little Campbell River.

After 1992, LFN's role shifted from lobbyist to caretaker. First on the agenda was to create a dual-use trail for both equestrians and pedestrians that would include two wide, sturdy bridges over the river. Supported by other groups, LFN applied for and received grant money to cover costs. The South Regional Trail was completed in 1994.

When Irene Pearce passed away four years later, the LFN lobbied the Township to have part of the trail officially named after her. This became a reality in 2000. Later, the LFN planted a Yellow Cedar tree beside the trail in her memory. A plaque was added to inform the general public of the tree's history. LFN members also adopted the Irene Pearce Trail under the Township's Adopt-a-Trail program, keeping it litter-free for many years.

Above: The dual-use trail is used by both equestrians and walkers, heading out to enjoy nature. Photos: Anthea Farr

Being a caretaker requires vigilance. In 2009, the LFN noticed a large pile of uncapped manure close to the Little Campbell River, in the hay field beside the park. A series of complaints were made to the Provincial Ministry of Environment regarding suspected pollution of a salmon spawning stream. This action eventually led to the removal of the manure pile. In 2021, a section of the river by the eastern bridge dried up during the unprecedented heat dome. Another warning to take climate change seriously!

If Irene could see the park now, we think she would be pleased. The Douglas-fir trees have grown taller and more majestic. Trails that wind through the forest provide opportunities to wonder or to find peacefulness. Langley Field Naturalists can be grateful that saner heads prevailed and granted park status to this cherished natural area.

Muskrat. The Municipal Natural Park can offer occasional glimpses of a muskrat or beaver swimming down the river. Photo: John Gordon

Hope Redwoods Natural Area
BY PHIL HENDERSON & BOB PULS

Larry Hope considered carefully the best use for the land that was his green space as a child.

He believed it was vital to keep the land green for future generations and abhorred the idea that it could be swallowed up by development.

Family was at the heart of Larry's decision to create The Redwoods Golf Course and its name reflects this. The name comes from the California Redwoods (*Sequoia sempervirens*) that his grandfather planted on the property in 1909 and 1910. These massive trees now line the south side of 96 Avenue, east of 216th Street. Larry planted additional redwoods at the golf course entrance off 88th Avenue. The importance of family is forever etched in The Redwoods logo of six trees: Larry, the large tree at the top, sheltering and protecting five smaller trees below, his daughters. Larry dedicated The Redwoods and its green space to the pioneers of Langley.

The Natural Area abuts the golf course. Photo: John Gordon

I (Phil) first met Larry when I approached him about conducting bird surveys in a young plantation of hybrid poplars he had planted at the south end of the property, next to the field where a few cattle grazed. The plantation had caught my eye while driving along 88th Avenue, so I tracked down the property's owner and arranged to meet him. I was new to the area and knew nothing about Larry, his family, or the history of the property, and was pleasantly surprised that he was most receptive to my idea. However, he insisted on one condition: "You can conduct bird surveys of the poplar plantation so long as you survey the whole property."

What surprised me more than the revised scope of study was the manner of how he said it: pragmatically, sternly, matter-of-factly. Larry was a serious fellow who expected hard work, dedication, and results, because—I realized—these are what he demanded of himself. He was a man of his word: honest, forthright, no-nonsense.

His humour and smile were often subtle. I saw his playful side, and his desire to engage with and help the community, during the annual Redwoods Halloween fireworks display. There he convincingly played a scary but likeable scarecrow, who cheerfully and ghoulishly greeted all the families, welcoming them to his property. I think his smile and exuberance stemmed from knowing the proceeds of this event all went to charity.

While I studied the birds and others studied fish, Larry studied the trees on the property. He received his BSc in Forestry from UBC in 1955, and was right at home conducting an inventory of the trees and getting to know his land a little better. He wanted to learn all he could about the natural history of the property.

Larry set a fine example for development and developers. He took an environment-first approach. He asked, "How could he develop the property and maintain its important natural features?"

Top: Colourful fungi. Photo: Anthea Farr
Bottom Left: Pacific Sideband Snail. Photo: Bob Puls
Bottom Right: Hairy Woodpecker. Photo: John Gordon

The identification and protection of the property's important natural features guided the golf course design and its development. Large pockets of trees remained on the periphery and on islands between fairways. Slowly, additional trees were removed as required, based on observations of conditions, safety, and the golfing experience. His stepwise development plan involved learning and adjusting as required over time.

Top Left: *Larry Hope. Photo: Langley Advance Times archives*
Bottom Left: *The Redwoods Golf Course logo*
Right: *Hope Redwoods Trail. Photo: Phil Henderson*

These efforts much impressed the Provincial Environment Office, as can be seen from this fax sent to Larry: "Redwoods is the most environmentally-friendly golf course I know of. Thanks for all your efforts to protect the habitat on your property."

In 2006, Larry Hope sold The Redwoods Golf Course to the Township of Langley at a price well below market value, with the condition that it would always remain as green space. Shortly after its purchase, the Township identified a seven acre (2.8 hectare) patch of remnant forest on the property (north of the golf course), to be designated as parkland.

In September 2007, the Langley Field Naturalists were asked by the Township of Langley to provide input on the location of a nature trail in the newly acquired parkland. To do this, the LFN conducted a bio-inventory in different seasons to identify the area's plant, bird, mammal, amphibian, reptile, and invertebrate species. The results of these surveys were presented in a report to the Township, along with the LFN's recommendations. The Township agreed with the LFN that the section was too small and fragile to be opened to the public and would be served only by a trail along the pipeline right-of-way which formed the southern boundary of this section.

The official name of this parkland is the Hope Redwoods Natural Area. Plants and animals in the forest have been left to thrive, undisturbed, but can still be appreciated by walkers and those wishing to sit on LFN's donated bench and "take it all in." At the start of the trail is a plaque honouring the history of the Hope family and acknowledging Larry's important role and contribution.

At the dedication of Hope Redwoods Natural Area in 2008, Larry spoke these concluding words:

> "... it makes us feel good knowing that down the road, many generations of families will have the opportunity to enjoy a beautiful park in their community. I believe the Mayor and Council should be complimented on their long-term vision to leave green spaces for future generations in Langley."

Left: Larry Hope by the interpretive sign at Hope Redwoods Natural Area. Photo: Daile Hawley
Right: LFN donated bench. Photo: Bob Puls

Mountain View Crown Lands
BY BOB PULS

"An almighty screeching and commotion occurred in the forest as I was standing beside the house of the late George and Bunty Clements. What on earth was all that noise? I stealthily walked towards the sounds and came across a Cooper's Hawk and a Barred Owl engaged in a verbal battle, most of the screeching coming from the hawk. I wasn't sure if it was a territorial dispute or a disagreement over prey, but I had never heard anything like it before."

The battle was taking place on land that I was getting to know well, a beautiful mixed forest in north Langley. Encompassing 62.7 hectares, this forest contains vernal ponds and a salmon stream (Davidson Creek). In short, it is land that could be viewed as a naturalist's paradise.

Barred Owl. Photo: Bob Puls

The story began like this.

In 2008, Malcolm Weatherston, Director of Development for the Mountain View Conservation Society (MVCS) and Gordon Blankstein, the owner of MVCS's land, approached the Langley Field Naturalists with a request. Would we conduct a biodiversity survey on the Crown land they were leasing, located next to the MVCS property? Although MVCS was involved mainly with raising endangered African wildlife, they also had some endangered Canadian species, including a small herd of bison and breeding colonies of Vancouver Island Marmots, Oregon Spotted Frogs and Northern Spotted Owls. Malcolm and Gordon wanted to know how they might be able to use the leased land to benefit endangered species.

This leased land became known as the Mountain View Crown Lands. Some folks previously knew it as the Dominion Sawmill site. It is bounded by 240th Street to the east, the old BC Rail line to the south, the CN railway line to the west and the MVCS land to the north. The beauty and appeal of the site evolved after the forest fire of 1917, which wiped out the sawmill. There was no sign of any past agricultural activities.

Not surprisingly, the LFN agreed to conduct the survey. We discovered that this site was also the last retreat for renowned naturalist Glenn Ryder, a founding LFN member described in earlier chapters. As well as doing a bio-inventory, Glenn was doing an industrial archaeological survey. He willingly shared his historical data, dating back to 1969, with the LFN.

The LFN's bio-inventory of the site began in 2009, with members blazing trails to extend those maintained by Glenn Ryder and neighbours George and Bunty Clements of Fur-Bearer Society fame. One of the first visits to the site happened after a snowfall

A Black Bear caught on a trail camera. Photo: Bob Puls
Inset: Report produced by the LFN for the Mountain View
Conservation Society.

had coated every twig and every branch, all gleaming white in winter sunshine. The snow, plus the Clements' many bird feeders attracting all kinds of birds and squirrels, led one LFN member to remark that "it was like stepping into Narnia."

The study lasted ten years and used various types of inventory methods, including moth traps, sweep nets and trail cameras. The latter recorded a black bear ambling down one of our trails. Regrettably, the iNaturalist website did not exist at that time, so experts were consulted to assist with identification of some of the more challenging species. Once the inventory ended, the LFN produced a 190-page report.*

What did we find? As expected, the site had high biodiversity. A total of approximately 1,638 species were identified over the

---

*Report on the Ten-Year Biodiversity Study of Langley Township's Mountain View Conservation Society's Leased Crown Land – 2009-2018: Langley Field Naturalists Society, Anthea Farr & Bob Puls.

10-year study: 150 vertebrate, 649 invertebrate, 404 plant, 405 fungi and six protozoa species. Another 40 species were recorded by Glenn Ryder prior to the study and many more specimens were photographed (2,275 photos) and/or collected (16 vials in 70% alcohol) which still have yet to be classified. During the 10-year period, 11 species at-risk, including Northern Red-legged Frogs, were recorded by various individuals. The long time span of the study was significant, as various species, particularly some fungi, only appeared once and were not seen again.

Two invertebrate species (spiders) found on the site were identified by the Royal British Columbia Museum as species found nowhere else in Canada. As well as having high biodiversity and rare or at-risk species, the forest acts as a significant carbon sink, helping to mitigate the effects of climate change.

The site also has historical and archaeological values. Evidence of a possible First Nations' pit house can be seen on the escarpment above the creek.

Top: Orange Honeysuckle
Photo: Bob Puls
Bottom: Black-tailed doe
with her piebald fawn.
Photo: Bob Puls
(trail camera)

The Langley Field Naturalists have strongly recommended that the site be protected, designated as a Conservation Area or as an Ecological Reserve, but to date the site has not been given protective status.

How will this be resolved? Probably not quickly, like the "discussion" between the hawk and the owl. Governments are renowned for their slow response—staff change, Ministries change, files get lost in the shuffle. Projects don't fit exactly into the current government's ideas and directives, and excuses for lack of progress are abundant. We can but hope that appropriate action to protect the site will be forthcoming.

Top Left: Hooker's Fairybells in flower. Photo: Bob Puls
Bottom Left: Red-legged Frog. Photo: Wim Vesseur
Right: Death Cap Mushroom. Photo: Bob Puls

Milaster Passive Park
BY ANTHEA FARR & BOB PULS

"This is a creek that likes to boogie."

— LISA DREVES, 2020

Lisa is right. Looking at the Township of Langley's aerial photos taken over two decades, we can see that Nathan Creek frequently changes its course. It is a creek that seems to have a mind of its own. Soon we would experience this first-hand.

We are standing on the banks of Nathan Creek that is located on a 40 acre (16 hectare) property in northeast Langley. The Township bought this property from Karl Milaster with the intention that one day it would be open to the public as a *passive* park.

Nathan Creek in Milaster Passive Park. Photo: Anthea Farr

Karl was given a lifetime residency agreement. The property also includes the creek's floodplain, where Red Alders and Black Cottonwoods flourish, plus steep wooded sections of the Glen Valley escarpment, where Big-leaf Maples thrive. At the southern end is the Trans Mountain pipeline right-of-way, which is kept clear of trees and shrubs.

After Karl died in 2017, the property became accessible for park development. In 2019, Lisa Dreves (LFN President) and Bob Puls (LFN Past President and Conservation Chair) toured the site with Al Neufeld (Township Parks Manager), who had asked if the LFN would do a bio-inventory of the property. Later that year, we received formal permission which allowed us to create access trails to begin our survey.

Gareth Pugh, Ryan Usenik, Ted and Lynda Lightfoot, Mike Klotz, Bob Puls, Lisa Dreves, Tom Wildeboer, and Herman Vanderleest were our trail blazers. It was hard work. Eventually,

Left: Raccoon. Photo: Eric Habisch
Right: LFN stairway to old logging road. Photo: Bob Puls

they established a route to the pipeline and the southern boundary in the lowland, plus a loop trail (using old logging roads) to the top of the escarpment at the north and east boundaries. This involved building a temporary bridge across the creek to access the meadow on the west side. It also included building a deluxe set of wooden stairs to access the start of the northern logging road. During this process, the trail blazers noted all species encountered.

With Bob's excellent leadership and record-keeping, the bio-inventory began in earnest in spring of 2020. By then, the Township had hired a contractor to remove the old house and all the trash associated with human occupation. We were free to explore and discover.

Species were determined using visual, audio and photographic clues, augmented by a bat detector and a trail camera. Sampling of invertebrates included use of sweep nets, Berlese funnels (for extraction from leaf litter) and a moth trap. Bob Puls, Anthea Farr and Corey Bunnell handled most of the observations but invaluable help with birds was provided by Gareth Pugh, Wim Vesseur and Eric Habisch who completed bird surveys at least once a month.

Aquatic surveys in the creek were conducted by staff from LEPS (Langley Environmental Partners Society), experts at identifying freshwater life forms. The iNaturalist website was helpful for identifying many other species, particularly insects. Spiders were identified by Claudia and Darren Copely and Dr. Rob Bennett at the Royal BC Museum. Their help was greatly appreciated.

Some of the things we have learned so far:

Standing on the banks of Nathan Creek, we now know that the creek can shrink and grow dramatically, rising 1 or 2 meters after a heavy rainfall. Our first plank bridge and then its successor were both washed out. An atmospheric river event (such as in

Fawn Lilies at Milaster. Photo: Corey Bunnell

November 2021) makes the creek "boogie." It boogied eastward; where we once stood on dry sand is now deep water. And yes, it is flowing over and into our gumboots!

We also learned that salmon use both the creek and its backwaters, and that black bear, beaver, otter, mink, muskrat, raccoon, deer, and coyote leave their tracks and scat along the sandy shoreline. High above the creek in the spring, insect-filled air provides important food for migrating swallows.

When we cleared brush from around a formerly invisible donut shaped vernal pond, we learned it was permanent, not vernal, with a pool of deep water that housed salamanders. We know that there are several species-at-risk here, including Oregon Forestsnails and Red-legged Frogs. Near the house site is a large patch of lovely White Fawn Lilies, which we believe Karl nurtured.

We also know that there are at least 818 animal species and 461 plant or fungal species here, because Bob has fastidiously recorded them all. Those numbers will likely increase. The inventory continues.

The Beetle Project
BY ANTHEA FARR

Inside a large tent, we are sucking up beetles. Wearing contraptions with clear tubes hanging out of our mouths, we home in on the densest clusters of beetles. Like some kind of alien anteater, each of us "sucks." Only, to my relief, the sucked-up beetles go into a bottle, not into my mouth. The scene is bizarre enough that it has been brought to the attention of the local press. What has made us behave like anteaters?

To be truthful, anteaters snack mostly on ants, not beetles. There is no doubt, however, that our behaviour looks odd. But we are under the supervision of Madlen Denoth, UBC PhD zoology

Above: Anthea Farr collects beetles for the Purple Loosestrife Project.
Photo: LFN Archives
Inset: Purple Loosestrife. Photo: Anthea Farr

student, and have carefully raised these beetles for one reason: to control a stubborn, invasive plant.

Our target is a patch of purple at Brydon Pond, located in the Nicomekl floodplain southeast of Brydon Lagoon. The purple is Purple Loosestrife (*Lythrum salicaria*); its tall pinkish-purple flower spikes look attractive to people and to bees. If only this plant knew its place, and stayed in it, we might not be so concerned. Unfortunately, it doesn't.

Originally from Asia and Europe, it spreads "like wildfire", choking out our native wetland plants and eliminating habitat for native fish and wildlife. Worse, one plant can produce up to 3 million seeds, seeds that can remain viable in the mud for up to 20 years. It's small wonder this species has earned the labels of "highly invasive" or "noxious weed" in North America.

Our beetles, small and brown, are *Galerucella calmariensis* and yes, they are approved biological control agents. Native to

Beetle Project (follow the leader, Madlen Denoth). Photo: LFN Archives

Europe, they eat only Purple Loosestrife. In fact, they excel at eating Purple Loosestrife and have successfully controlled it at other locations, including Jericho Beach Park in Vancouver and Iona Beach Regional Park in Richmond.

But how did the Langley Field Naturalists end up in these tents? In 2000, LFN members Rhys and Annabel Griffiths helped spearhead this beetle project. The first few summers, the beetles were fed and bred in two large tents at Trinity Western University, under UBC's supervision. In 2003, the tents needed a new home. LFNers Joan and Ron Wilmshurst kindly responded, allowing the two tents to sit on the lawn of their lovely south Langley acreage. The welfare of the beetles then became our responsibility.

Bumble Bee on a native wild rose. A variety of native plants can provide food for bees from early spring to late fall. In contrast, Purple Loosestrife chokes out native plants and provides "bee food" for only a short period.
Photo: Joanne Rosenthal

Months later, we are surrounded by beetles. Each tent contains a plastic wading pool filled with water and pots of loosestrife. Joan and Ron carefully tended these all summer, from June to August. The 200 beetles brought here from Iona have thrived. Whenever they needed more food, emergency trips were made to loosestrife sites to collect more plant stalks to keep them going. Sure enough, under this dedicated care, the beetles have mated and multiplied. The tents now house about 3,000 of them.

The inside of this tent is getting hotter. After all, it is August. Finally, we have collected pretty much all of the beetles for the next and final step. Off to Brydon Pond! There the beetles are released to do their job—eat to their heart's content...

Years later: We can really see the difference this project made at Brydon Pond. Any loosestrife that still rears its stalk out of the mud has severely nibbled leaves, full of holes. The university students even have data (such as stem counts and heights) plus photos, to quantify the impact the beetles have had. Best of all, when we look underneath those nibbled leaves, we can still find beetles that will keep nibbling.

In 2004, there was an unexpected reward. The judges of the federal Communities in Bloom competition were debating which community (in the 20 to 50 thousand population category) should win first prize; there were several that were close, all sporting beautiful flower gardens. Another criterion was a community's environmental awareness. Finally, the judges made their decision: Langley City. What was the one thing that swayed them to choose Langley City? The beetle project!

POSTSCRIPT
We didn't stop with our success at Brydon Pond. With permission, we also released beetles to control Purple Loosestrife in a wetland behind Twin Rinks arena on the Langley Bypass and in Aldergrove Regional Park near 0 Avenue.

The Beetle Project was very much a collaborative effort. We are grateful to:

LFN members who helped with paperwork and/or beetle collecting, raising and releasing: Rhys and Annabel Griffiths, Joan and Ron Wilmshurst, Phil Henderson, Keith Robertson, Anthea Farr and other willing helpers.

UBC: Dr. Judith Myers, Zoology professor, her PhD student, Madlen Denoth, and student assistant Jennifer Passmore. Madlen supervised and took part in all aspects of the project.

Trinity Western University: for providing the initial site for the beetle tents as well as students to help collect beetles.

Metro Vancouver (then known as GVRD): for granting permission to collect beetles from Iona Beach Regional Park.

City of Vancouver: for granting permission to collect beetles from Jericho Beach Park.

Canadian Tire in Langley: for donating funds to purchase the tents and for providing employees to help with collection of beetles.

Mountain Equipment Co-op & Canada's ecoAction 2000: for providing funding for Madlen Denoth to use on this project.

City of Langley Parks Department: for support and for sending a truck at the end of the summer to the Wilmshurst's to collect the remaining plants for incineration.

BC Ministry of Agriculture, Fisheries and Food: Mr. Roy Cranston, Weed Specialist, for his cooperation.

Canadian Purple Loosestrife Biocontrol Agent (in Manitoba): Cory Lindgren, for project approval and forms.

The beetles: for doing what they were supposed to do.

CHAPTER 6

The Eco Reserve: Fraser River Tales

by Anthea Farr

The current is so strong. I stop staring at it and tell myself: We LFNers are strong paddlers. Check: Are our lifejackets tightly strapped on? Yes. We nose our canoe into the water, carefully step in, and begin to paddle, hard. *Stroke, stroke, stroke.* There is no pausing or the mighty Fraser will take us west—too far west! We are totally focused on our paddling. *Stroke, stroke, stroke.* All the way across. Finally, we reach our destination: the ever-so-welcome shore of the Fraser River Islands Ecological Reserve. As I step onto the sand, I feel relief, gratitude and the familiar anticipation. What will we find this time?

But first, "How on earth did we end up doing this?" To answer that, we need to backtrack decades to acknowledge one man with a vision: Vladimir Krajina. A WWII hero who fled Czechoslovakia, Krajina was destined to become a legendary professor in UBC's Forestry Faculty. Thanks to him, BC was divided into BEC (Biogeoclimatic Ecosystem Classification) zones, a system still widely used today.

Another goal of Krajina's was to set aside reserves, representing each BEC zone and sub-zone. This is still a work in progress, but it began when the Ecological Reserve Act was enacted in 1971 (there are now 148 reserves in BC). These vital reserves were also chosen to protect rare species and special features of biological or geological importance and to be used for scientific study and educational purposes.

Facing: ER 76 on a sunny fall day. Photo: Anthea Farr

Founding LFN member Ray Gurr (left) and first ER warden Dan Rempel (right) on the reserve. They accompanied me on almost every visit to these islands, providing invaluable help. Photo: Anthea Farr

Fast forward to 1981, when Lynne Milnes, Warden Program Coordinator for Ecological Reserves (ER), came to our LFN general meeting with a request. The LFN was the closest naturalist club to ER 76, also known as the Cottonwood Islands or Fraser River Islands, situated just west of Chilliwack. Back then, Abbotsford and Chilliwack naturalist clubs did not exist. ER 76 consisted of the last unaltered and "uncommitted" floodplain islands in the lower Fraser. Unlike most other islands along the Fraser, these had cottonwoods that would never be turned into toilet paper.

Lynne's question was: "Would one of us be a volunteer warden for ER 76?" Ever the willing volunteer, Dan Rempel said "Yes!". Other LFN members, including Herb Pastrick, Bill Knowlson and Ray Gurr, offered to help in whatever ways they could.

One thing became apparent. Getting to these islands would be the greatest challenge. A litany of problems surfaced, including the following: The strong current broke the shear pin on Herb Pastrick's outboard motor boat; on another memorable trip, four canoeists got very wet; a cedar canoe was lost (whether taken from a gravel bar by the wind or by humans, we still don't know). Yes, we made mistakes, but at least we learned from those mistakes.

Another challenge came from the islands themselves: they are "shape-shifters". They keep growing on one side and shrinking on the other side. And between the islands is a channel that changes; it can be dry sand or deep water. We never knew what to expect.

Despite these challenges, Dan (1st warden) and myself (2nd warden) took our warden duties seriously and forged on. We posted ER signs, collected washed-up garbage, recorded species of flora and fauna, beaver activities and signs of human use (violations were thankfully rare, but we did find evidence of hunting, fishing, camping, tree cutting, etc.).

Top: Posting signs was one of a warden's duties. Photo: LFN Archives
Bottom: Dan Rempel (1st warden) by a beaver-felled Black Cottonwood tree. Photo: Anthea Farr

Each time we stepped onto the shore we knew—at that moment in time—we were the only people on those islands. What a privilege! We were greeted only by bird song and the rustling of the breeze in the cottonwood leaves. At our feet, the wet sand, riddled with tracks, told us stories and which birds and mammals might be residents or perhaps just visitors: a Great Blue Heron, Canada Geese, beavers, deer... And how interesting it was to witness the "shapeshifting". On one side, fierce erosion was undercutting banks, toppling large cottonwood trees. On the other side, gentle sand beds were growing, edged with ribbons of horsetails, shrubs and young cottonwoods.

Top: Ray Gurr walking by the eroding shoreline.
Bottom: Vegetation zones along shoreline.
Facing: Pink Salmon. Photos: Anthea Farr

LFN members eagerly read about our trips in the club's newsletters. ER headquarters filed our reports and sometimes offered advice. First Dan and then myself attended the annual wardens' meetings, held in different areas in the province. There we learned much about the problems other wardens were dealing with and how they were trying to solve them. Our access challenges were unique, but at least they kept unwanted human incursions to a minimum.

In 1987, I thought the access problem was solved when Federal Fisheries agreed to ferry us to the reserve on their jet boat, during their annual river trip to Hope, then pick us up on their return. And for a few years, it worked like a charm. So fast and effortless! Then the day came when they told us they were going to reduce fuel costs, by going one way to Hope in their jet boat and returning by vehicle. If we waited for the jet boat to return, we would be on the islands for a year! Sometime after that, I "passed the torch" to warden #3, Bev Ramey of Nature Vancouver. She and her husband, both experienced kayakers, were able to meet all of the challenges.

I smell the fish before I see them. Every second year, pink salmon spawn along the shorelines of the Fraser River, laying eggs that will become the next generation. Here on the reserve, I believe these eggs are safer than most, less likely to be disturbed by humans. I breathe deeply, proud that the LFN have played a role in caring for this Ecological Reserve. The Fraser River Islands will remain a surprising—yet worthwhile—part of our stewardship history.

CHAPTER 7

On the Trail:
Field Trips

by Sheila Puls & Anthea Farr

> *"In every walk with nature,*
> *one receives far more than he seeks."*
>
> **– JOHN MUIR**

The trail is a naturalist's *happy place*. One could say that walks or hikes, known as Field Trips, form the essential core of the LFN. Photos taken in the 1970s and 80s show that elements of field trips have changed little over the past 50 years. They include planning and poring over maps (perhaps the clothes have changed and the maps might be on cell phones now), gathering at the trip's starting point (the cars have definitely changed), bringing out the scopes and binoculars, and heading down the trail.

These walks can last one or two hours, a half-day, a full day or multiple days (the latter with campsites or motels pre-booked). Destinations range from local parks and natural areas to parks and nature reserves in other parts of BC. Excerpts from old LFN newsletters provide a glimpse of what it was like to explore nature "on the trail".

Evening Walks

The shortest LFN walks are the Wednesday evening summer walks, when the heat of the day dissipates and the cooler air of evening gradually moves in. Birds become quieter but mammals and frogs may awaken, showing themselves to the

Facing: 2010 Salt Spring Island intertidal beach walk. Photo: Anne Gosse

most fortunate observers. In 1981, destinations for summer evening walks were as follows: Campbell Valley Regional Park, Brydon Lagoon, Sendall Gardens, Aldergrove Regional Park, Golden Ears Provincial Park, Redwood Park, Allard Crescent and Forslund-Watson Wildlife Area. Here is how Trudy Pastrick summarized some highlights of those 1981 walks:

> *"July was a very active month with many families of young birds on ponds, or in their nests, like the Pied-billed Grebe and young American Coots at the sewage pond (Brydon Lagoon), young Black-headed Grosbeaks at Redwood Park, a nest full of Cedar Waxwings at Campbell Valley Park. A rare discovery of the gnome plant in its prime colour of yellow or pale pink, was seen on the Spirea Trail at Golden Ears Park. Many other wildflowers were at their best, plants such as the ox-eyed daisy, sundew, cottongrass, lovely long spikes of the foxgloves, twinflowers, etc., growing alongside the trail. Mats of feathery mosses added a certain freshness to the woods."*

Brydon Lagoon at dusk. Photo: John Gordon

"Birds of a Feather Flock Together"

Moving on to the "regular" field trips, we can discern from club newsletters that the focus of these ranged from birding to botany, from fish to fungi, and so on. We begin with a birding trip, always popular, at one of the premier destinations for those who love birds.

George C. Reifel Migratory Bird Sanctuary, November 2001

"The skies cleared and the sun shone on our walk in the Reifel Bird Sanctuary. Eight of us enjoyed seeing the thousands of snow geese feeding along the shoreline and lifting into the sky with their loud alarm calls whenever threatened by an eagle or hawk. These geese feed at the shoreline when the tide is out, coming into the fields at night or at high tide. From their breeding grounds on Wrangel Island off the coast of Siberia, they begin coming to Reifel in September, reaching peak numbers in November. We counted 31 species of birds and had two highlights: a beautiful Barred Owl, easily seen perched near a path, and two Black-crowned Night-Herons, one of which was clearly visible—they are usually tucked in the shrubbery." – Joan Wilmshurst

Black-crowned Night-Heron. Photo: John Gordon

Fish & Fungi

Though some may find this hard to believe, some naturalists like fish more than birds. The same can be said about fungi. Here are examples of a *fish trip* and a *fungi trip*.

Weaver Creek Spawning Channel, October 1997

"After we arrived at the spawning channel, we picked up explanatory brochures and spent the next couple of hours watching the fish in the channel. It was interesting to try to figure out which of the three spawning species we were seeing. Sockeyes were the easiest to recognize because of their bright red and green colour, but after a short time we were able to identify the other two species, chum and pink, as well. It really is amazing to watch them spawning.

This well-planned project was put in place to save a valuable run of sockeye that was declining drastically because of logging and natural intermittent flooding of the creek. Since the building of the channel, the commercial catch of salmon from this creek has increased dramatically. The human-made and controlled channel imitates and enhances the natural environment these fish need in order to reproduce. As we saw, it has been very successful." – Arnold Code

Golden Ears Provincial Park, September 2018

"A fine day for our fungus discovery walk in Golden Ears Provincial Park, with Anthea, Christina (from Burke Mountain Naturalists) plus two guests joining Jude and I. At our meeting spot, Jude discovered a population of beautiful earthstars (nice fresh ones). Then we headed straight for the Lower Falls Trail which follows Gold Creek. The only gold in Gold Creek as far as I can see is a golden opportunity to enjoy nature in this lovely valley. The Vine Maple leaves were very beautiful and the mushrooms plentiful. A few of our discoveries were: Zeller's Bolete, Blackening Russula, Honey Mushroom, Bristly Pholiota, a milk cap (Lactarius sp.), Jelly fungus, Sulphur Tuft, an Inky cap, Maple leaf tar spot, Pink coral (spotted by Anthea), very beautiful, Bird's nest fungus, Turkey Tail." – Al Grass

Left: Al Grass finding fungi. Photo: Anne Gosse
Right: Inky cap fungi. Photo: Anthea Farr

Green & Leafy

There are also some naturalists keen to become better acquainted with plants. Here are two examples of walks that focused on botany: one on bog plants, the other on trees.

Derby Reach Bog, August 1999

"Under clear skies, a group of about ten of us explored the bog in Derby Reach Regional Park, an area not yet open to the general public. We examined some of the interesting vegetation within the bog (Tawny Cottongrass, White Beak-rush, Sphagnum, blueberries and cranberries) growing beside the hog fuel trails. We were thrilled by the return of five Common Nighthawks on this second annual bog foray. As it grew darker, the nighthawks dove and swooped lower, foraging for insects. We also spotted two Coyotes in the bog, not far off the trails." – Phil Henderson

Left: Sundew is a carnivorous bog plant. Sticky drops on its leaves attract insects, which become trapped and are then slowly devoured. Photo: Anthea Farr
Right: Skunk cabbage, a common wetland plant. Photo: Bob Puls

2012 LFN group posing in a shady grove. Photo: Anne Gosse

Riverview Arboretum, April 2012

"*Seven LFN members joined our tour leader and her helper at Riverview Arboretum for a very informative morning on the lovely spacious grounds of Riverview Hospital. We were shown many different types of beautiful trees that had been planted and nurtured—some 100 years ago! We were told that for 60 years, only two expert gardeners were responsible for all the work of grafting, planting and developing this lovely 98 hectare horticultural park. Some of the magnificent tree specimens were the huge Silver Lindens, native to Europe, Gingko Biloba trees and Dawn Redwoods from China, Atlas Cedars from North Africa, Sitka Spruce and many lovely blooming Magnolia trees. These are just a hint of what we were shown.*" – Anne Gosse

A Hardy Bunch

Sometimes conditions on the trail are not to everyone's, or even anyone's, liking. Here are two examples that prove that Langley Field Naturalists can be a hardy bunch.

Stanley Park Field Trip, November 1991

"It was one of our wettest and windiest days. Some members obviously were discouraged by reports of the park closure due to the severe conditions. Those hardy members who got soaked in the torrential rain sighted 45 species of presumably equally hardy birds. Leader Mike would like to see this trip re-scheduled." – LFN Archives

2016. A group enjoying more pleasant weather on a walk.
Photo: LFN Archives

West Creek Wetlands, July 2018

"*Several brave souls headed out into West Creek Wetlands Regional Park Preserve; they took only pictures but left far more than their footprints. Thanks to their sacrifice, thousands of mosquitoes went to bed with full tummies that night.*

West Creek Wetlands never fails to disappoint BUT the mosquitoes made this evening walk almost unbearable. Stopping for any length of time to learn about the abandoned wasabi farm, marvelling at the grove of cascara that remains, or gazing out at the beauty of Wood Duck Lake meant dozens of bloodthirsty creatures would descend upon you, and then they called their friends.

The riot of bird calls and Douglas Squirrel trills was probably in thanks to us brave souls taking the mosquitoes' attention away, allowing them to go about their bird and squirrel business. Only one beaver tail smack was heard at the wetland, the family probably choosing to stay inside their lodge, away from the mosquitoes." – Lisa Dreves

EDITOR'S NOTE
West Creek Wetlands is not open to the public, so special permission to access the property must be obtained from Metro Vancouver Parks. (Usually, it is a wonderful place to visit.)

"Five Star" Ratings

Not that anyone is rating these trips, but sometimes everything seems perfect: the weather, the sightings, the sounds and the company. Below are two such outings.

Skagit Valley, September 2007

"Al and Jude led 14 keen naturalists into Skagit Valley Provincial Park as far as Ross Lake. At our first stop at Silver Lake, we were awed with the sight of an osprey swooping down to snatch a fish. We watched for several minutes as he laboriously circled higher and higher up the mountainside to his lofty perch while carrying his heavy load.

At our next stop beside the Skagit River Bridge, we found Wild Ginger and Vanilla-leaf and Al explained the interesting slave/master relationship of lichens on some of the nearby trees. After that we enjoyed lunch at Ross Lake Picnic Area where a flock of brightly coloured Red Crossbills gave us a great sighting (revealing their crossed bills in our scopes as well!). A golden gleaming American Kestrel dropped by to check us out. Our day finished with a meander through Chittenden Meadow to view the unique Ponderosa Pines area and discover many interesting fungi on the return walk —which Al took great delight in."– Anne Gosse

Hayward Lake Recreation Area, May 1994

"Delightful sights and sounds greeted the 15 naturalists at Hayward Lake Recreation Area. A male Red-breasted Sapsucker beat his bill on the metal of a lamp standard as he called to his mate. Another pair repeated this action further along the trail. Wood Duck babies followed their mother along the edge of a sheltered pond, while Red-winged Blackbirds filled the air with their melodious songs.

An Osprey rode the wind currents over the trees and the lake. The seldom seen Green Heron slowly moved along the edge of the shore while a pair of Cinnamon Teal drifted among the reeds. A female Rufous Hummingbird flitted by on her business of collecting soft dry cattail heads for her nest. "How are you? I am fine." The Solitary Vireo remained hidden among the trees and lush spring growth.

"Witchity, witchity, witchity, witch" came the call of the tiny Yellowthroat Warbler as we followed his movement among the bushes. These were only a few of the 28 species of birds seen and identified under the able leadership of Lynn Miller from the Central Valley Naturalists Club.

Yellow pond lilies, bleeding hearts, blue forget-me-nots and deep pink flowers of salmonberry gave bright spots of colour among the fresh greens of spring. A truly enjoyable outing."
– Irene Pearce

Surprise!

Surprises can happen anywhere. This trip had a surprising change of focus, followed by an even bigger surprise.

E. C. Manning Provincial Park, July 2021

"We embarked upon our normal loop walk around Heather Meadows and soon discovered a lack of birds and the flowers, although pretty, were greenish rather than the multiple colours we had seen in the past. So Eric, a butterfly enthusiast, soon had us all trying to photograph butterflies, which were numerous but far too active. Eventually, enough settled down and posed for a fair variety of pictures, with about 15 species being recorded.

After lunch, we headed for Strawberry Flats. Again, we concentrated on butterfly photography as we walked along the trail with Gareth in the lead. He had his head down, watching little Blues, until someone suggested he stop and back up! We were all close together, but I think Gareth's nose was fairly close to that of a black bear as we rounded a corner. The bear looked at us long enough for some photos and then ambled off to the side—this is when Wim said "I see another, and another," and we realised she had two cubs with her. Having reached our allotted time limit at this point, we turned around, ambled back to the cars and headed for home." – Bob Puls

Many thanks to all of the LFN Field Trip Coordinators for organizing diverse and amazing field trips over the past half century!

Photos: Anne Gosse

CHAPTER 8

Citizen Science: Valuable Data

by Anthea Farr, Bob Puls & Gareth Pugh

Citizen science is the practice of public participation and collaboration in scientific research to increase scientific knowledge.

— NATIONAL GEOGRAPHIC

The LFN takes part in a great many citizen science projects. While many of them involve counting, knowledge of the absence or presence of a species can also be useful to scientists as well as land use decision makers. Anyone who uses iNaturalist or eBird or another similar site is contributing to citizen science. But the line between conservation and citizen science can indeed be a blurry one. The LFN conservation projects, described in earlier chapters, all contain elements that could be inserted into this chapter.

Bird Counts

Langley Field Naturalists especially seem to like counting birds, and many of these counts have contributed to broader scientific knowledge. They include the Alouette and the White Rock Christmas Bird Counts, Backyard Bird Counts, Metro Vancouver Regional Park bird counts, Nighthawk & Nightjar Surveys in BC's interior, Spring Bird Surveys, Breeding Bird Surveys, Raptor Counts, Crow Counts—the list goes on.

Facing: Bob Puls cleaning out a nest box at Forslund-Watson.
Photo: Anne Gosse

"The crow count was so much more than just numbers. We had articles in the local paper that brought out individuals from all over Langley. Dozens of people connected to the wonder of birds and nature. Even on nights when we weren't there, people came to see the crows." — **LISA DREVES**

The first Christmas Bird Count (CBC) that LFN members probably took part in happened even before the club formed, on January 2, 1972. This inaugural White Rock CBC (all CBCs are 15-mile diameter circles) included part of Langley and a bit of northern Washington State. A North American tradition, the Audubon CBC was started by ornithologist Frank Chapman in 1900, as an alternative to shooting birds on Christmas Day.

Audubon Society records show the following details about the 1972 White Rock CBC. A total of 32 observers spent 80 hours counting birds and ended up with a total of 108 species and 17,125 individual birds. Nearly fifty years later, in the 2021 White Rock CBC, all of these numbers were higher. A total of 84 observers (plus 24 feeder watchers) spent 187 hours counting birds, ending up with a total of 112 species and 47,735 individual birds.

Such an increase in participants mirrors the growing interest in birdwatching. The important CBC data is used by Audubon, Bird Studies Canada, and other organizations to assess the health of bird populations. When combined with other surveys, such as the North American Breeding Bird Survey, this vital long-term perspective provides a picture of how the continent's bird populations have changed in time and space over more than a hundred years. A perspective that can help to protect birds and their habitat, it can also help to identify environmental issues—with implications for people as well.

CROW COUNT

This is the fourth time in February, 2022, that crow counters have stationed themselves along roads on all four sides of the roost. The sun has set; the sky is darkening. Bitterly cold, perhaps thinking about the after-count hot choc-

olate, the counters ready themselves. When the crows start to come, they come slowly at first and then, in dozens, hundreds, and thousands. Rivers of crows flow in from all over Langley, Surrey, Abbotsford, and south of the border to reach this south Aldergrove roost.

No one is sure why. To stay safe? To stay warm? To learn where food is? The crows aren't talking, at least not to us. They seem to be jockeying for position in their roost trees. The crows at the top could be picked off in the night by an owl. The ones at the bottom could be splattered with "whitewash" from the ones above... How many? The average of these four counts is an astounding 52,902. When this number was passed on to Dr. Rob Butler, British Columbia's authority on crows, he said that this roost is the largest crow roost in the Salish Sea! Citizen science can be chilly but oh-so-worthwhile.

Crows coming in to roost. Photo: Bob Puls

Nest Box Projects

Ryan Usenik checking a swallow box.
Photo: Anthea Farr

As well as counting birds, LFN members also seem to like to build, install and monitor bird nest boxes. Usually this is a case of wanting to help birds whose species may have lost their natural nest cavities due to forest clearing, or species that are declining or at risk for other reasons. Helping birds is a more common motive for building boxes than is contributing to science, although both can happen.

Like bird counts, nest box projects began as soon as, or even before, the LFN formed. Sometimes they were requested by landowners and other times, the LFN initiated them, obtaining permission from landowners. Boxes have been placed on many sites in Langley City and in the Township and each box is designed for a certain species: Swallow (Tree or Violet-green), Purple Martin, Screech-Owl, Barn Owl, Wood Duck, Chickadee (Black-capped or Chestnut-backed), etc.

All of the above-named species have raised healthy broods in our nest boxes. For example, swallows have used our boxes in Aldergrove Regional Park (Marvin's Marsh and Gordon's Brook), in Campbell Valley Regional Park (vernal wetland east of 200th Street), along the Glen Valley dyke, at or near Brydon Lagoon and at the Forslund-Watson Wildlife Reserve. Western Screech-Owls used our nest boxes at Forslund-Watson until about 2006. Barn Owls have used our box at Jackman Wetlands. Wood Ducks have used our boxes at Forslund-Watson and at Brydon Lagoon. Chickadees have used our boxes at Sendall Gardens and Doubleday Arboretum.

Above: John Ellens (left) and Glenn Ryder (right) with Western Screech-Owl nest boxes at Forslunds. Frugal out of necessity, Glenn initially made owl nest boxes using the wood from old dynamite crates. This seemed to work well. But when Glenn requested more from the manufacturer, he was told to STOP. "Don't hammer nails into a dynamite crate—it could explode!" Photo: Trudy Pastrick Inset: Western Screech-Owl. Photo: John Gordon

Sometimes other species have cashed in on these pre-built homes, surprising the naturalists who built them. These surprises can be nice, nasty, or simply groan-inducing. For example, the nice: an American Kestrel in a Wood Duck box, a Hooded Merganser in a Wood Duck box. The nasty: Yellowjackets or Paper Wasps (in any kind of box). The groan-inducing: House Sparrows, European Starlings, Deer Mice and, sometimes, House Wrens. Although uncommon in Langley, House Wrens are common and increasing in much of North America. In south Langley, House Wrens have commandeered swallow boxes, evicting the swallows and even their eggs. One male House Wren may "capture" as many as five swallow boxes in which he will build nests. From these, the female wren will choose which one she deems suitable for her eggs and offspring. Meanwhile, the swallows, whose numbers are declining, have lost five nesting locations.

And the science? Long-term records of nest box use in a certain area can be useful to scientists, as they can provide another way to verify that a trend is happening with a population, either an increase or a decline. Or, if scientists want to know what impact volunteers can have on a species-at-risk by putting up nest boxes, they need look no further than the example of the Purple Martin.

Purple Martin

The Purple Martin is a large member of the swallow family; the male is a deep glossy purplish-blue. Like the other swallows, it is an aerial insectivore, feeding exclusively on insects while flying. Other aerial insectivores include the swifts, flycatchers, nighthawks and poorwills. Much appreciated by bird-lovers, this group of birds also provides essential and free natural pest control services to farmers and communities.

*Above: Purple Martin nest boxes at
Tavistock Point, Brae Island. Photo: Bob Puls
Inset: Purple Martin. Photo: John Gordon*

But they are a group of birds that are in trouble.

Until 2006, the Purple Martin population in British Columbia was on the Red List (extirpated, endangered, or threatened). Declines had occurred throughout North America and they were thought to be human-caused. Humans introduced European Starlings and House Sparrows to North America, two species which readily took over the natural nest cavities used by the martins.

Fortunately, conservation groups here and elsewhere stepped in to help. The species is amenable to help, readily using human-made nest boxes put up near or over water. Martin houses have a long history. Some Native American tribes hung hollow gourds around their villages to attract these birds, probably to reduce mosquitoes or flies. Later, settlers copied them.

LFN decided to join the bandwagon of groups helping Purple Martins in the Lower Mainland. Working with LEPS and Metro Vancouver Parks, LFN members helped establish and then monitor Purple Martin nest boxes at Tavistock Point off Brae Island in the Fraser River. The boxes were in place in 2012 but patience was required. Finally, the martins accepted them, breeding in one box in 2018 and in more boxes in 2019. Then disaster struck in 2021!

During the spring freshet, when adult martins were busy feeding young, a log boom broke loose from its moorings upstream. It rammed the pilings the nest boxes were on, knocking the whole structure over and taking it down the Fraser River. Fortunately, the following year the martins showed their resilience. They moved into boxes placed at nearby Muench Bar, where two pairs fledged several chicks.

Today in BC, artificial nest boxes for Purple Martins account for almost all of their nests, with over 1,200 nesting pairs and 120 active colonies documented in the Lower Mainland and the east coast of Vancouver Island in recent years. The LFN helped the species expand its breeding range to include Langley. Thanks to a large number of dedicated groups, the species has been upgraded to Blue-listed (vulnerable) instead of endangered in BC. A success story indeed!

Purple Martins. Photo: Eric Habisch

Barn Owl box on the Nicomekl floodplain. Photo: Bob Puls

Barn Owl Nest Box Project

The Barn Owl is another species at risk in BC. Here in Langley, old wooden barns favoured by Barn Owls are becoming scarce. As noted in Chapter 3, the Forslund-Watson barn was destroyed by a storm and was never re-built. To offer alternative nest sites, the LFN installed some Barn Owl boxes in Langley, such as at The Redwoods Golf Course, Forslund-Watson, Brydon Lagoon and Jackman Wetlands Park.

These locations were selected because they were areas the club identified as having good foraging habitat for Barn Owls. Although so far only one of these boxes has been used by Barn Owls (Jackman Wetlands), we remain hopeful that more may be used in the years ahead.

Bald Eagle Nest Monitoring

When renowned Bald Eagle biologist David Hancock of the Hancock Wildlife Foundation put out a call for help in 2020, LFN members responded. David needed volunteers to monitor Bald Eagle nests in the Greater Vancouver area, which includes Surrey and Langley. The tasks were to try and make three visits to each nest: one early in the season to determine if the nest territory is active, a second visit to determine if the pair is on eggs or with small young, and a third visit to try and determine productivity—how many young are present and about to fledge.

If there is one thing LFNers love, it is raptors. Members eagerly stepped up to fill the void. Coordinated by Gareth Pugh, a number of eagle nests in Surrey or Langley were assigned to individuals or teams: Gareth himself, Anne Gosse, Caren Porter, Bob Puls, Tom Wildeboer, Wim Vesseur, Ted Goshulak, Ryan Usenik and three White Rock and Surrey Naturalists. That year, a total of 17 eaglets were recorded in the Langley nests and 32 in the Surrey nests. Although some nests were on private property where access was not possible, others were on properties where the owners were happy to allow access and to even help with the monitoring.

These eagle nest observations were added to the Hancock Wildlife Foundation's extensive and important database. Every eagle nest, occupied or unoccupied, and other raptor nests when occupied are protected by Section 34 of the BC Wildlife Act. However, this protection is largely dependent on citizens reporting concerns and potential infractions. The Foundation's database has played a key role in maintaining our eagle nests in the Greater Vancouver area.

What About Mammals?

Mammals have not been forgotten by the LFN nest box or survey crews. Under the enthusiastic guidance of Ryan Usenik, nest box programs expanded to include boxes for Flying Squirrels and for bats. The boxes were made and installed by club members, with materials paid for by the club. Locations for these boxes were chosen for their habitat suitability and, in some cases, for their visibility to the public, to hopefully increase public awareness of these species' importance.

In 2017 and 2018, bat boxes were installed at Brydon Lagoon, McMillan Island, and the Forslund-Watson Wildlife Area. In 2020, the LFN gratefully received a BC Nature grant to purchase a bat monitor with a compatible iPad. Since then, LFN members have assisted the BC Community Bat Program by monitoring two bat roosts in south Langley. Many of our conservation areas were also able to have bat surveys with these new tools. All of these surveys contribute to a better scientific understanding of bat populations in Langley.

Recently, the LFN installed Flying Squirrel nest boxes in the Municipal Natural Park. An iconic creature of the night, the Flying Squirrel (inset photo) has big black eyes, silky-soft gray fur, and flaps of skin that allow it to glide from tree to tree. Once fairly common, it may no longer exist here. When Barred Owls arrived and spread throughout Langley, they had Flying Squirrels on their menu. If these squirrels are still here, at least they now have more dwellings to choose from. The Municipal Natural Park also offers an abundance of fall fungi (aka squirrel food).

Photo: Gareth Pugh

CHAPTER 9

The Raptor Count: Eagles, Hawks, Falcons

by Anthea Farr

"There are still a few eagles around. I saw 10, mostly near the river in the Glen Valley Park area. Red-tailed Hawks are still not very common. I seldom see more than the ten that I saw this time. I did see three Northern Harriers which these days is unusual. The bonus sighting was at the very end of the count. I was approaching my vehicle at the last stop when a flash of white flew over my head and into a tree. Upon closer inspection, it was a Sharp-shinned Hawk. It looked at me briefly, then flew off and out of sight. So that concludes this season's count. The numbers this year I think are disappointing. But I always enjoy being out there, anticipating that next flash of white over my head." – **RAY GURR, MARCH 2005**

How It Began

In 1980, someone in the LFN suggested that we should conduct roadside raptor surveys. After all, the Vancouver Natural History Club had been doing them for years in Delta and in Pitt Meadows. Many habitats used by hawks and eagles were changing as development expanded and naturalists felt it was important to document how our raptors were coping. So it began—in November, 1980, the LFN completed their first survey for the Long-term Raptor Monitoring Project (aka the Raptor Count) which targeted nine raptors and an "odd-ball wannabe."

Did LFN members imagine that *long-term* would be as long as 26 years? I doubt it! But the raptor counters were a dedicated

Facing: American Kestrel. Photo: John Gordon

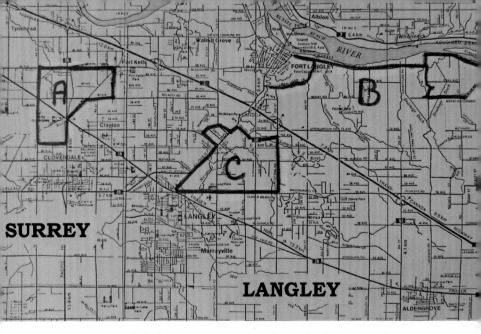

Areas A, B and C: the three survey areas chosen for the Raptor Count.
Map Source: Dominion Map Company

bunch, with a great fondness for birds—especially raptors. Three areas were chosen for the roadside surveys: Area A (Fry's Corner in Surrey), Area B (Fort Langley/Glen Valley) and Area C (Langley Airfield). Each area had about 40 km of roads from which raptors could be observed.

Objectives were:

1) to detect any significant trends in abundance of raptors,

2) to find out if cycles occurred with the more abundant species, and

3) to compare habitat use between the three survey areas.

Counts were conducted on the first weekend of each month from October to March, to include both migrating and wintering birds.

The Intrepid

Who were these intrepid raptor counters, out in all weathers—fair or foul? For almost all of this long-term survey, the same naturalists counted in the same areas. Two were LFN founding members: Mary Pastrick (assisted by her husband, Herb), who counted raptors in Area C and Ray Gurr, who counted raptors in Area B. Area A was adopted by member Dan Rempel, assisted by Bill Knowlson. Not surprisingly, all of these members were also active in many other LFN activities, as is often the case with hard-working volunteers who form the core of a club.

Two areas had different counters in the final years. In 2003, Area C was transferred to Phil Henderson and Roy Yates and in 2004, Area A was transferred to Joan Wilmshurst and Kathy Masse. Counts in these areas ended after the winter of 2004-5, due in part to the heavy traffic in Area A that was making raptor searches increasingly dangerous. Only Area B stayed with the same observer (Ray Gurr) for the entire project and included the winter of 2005-6.

Who else? All three areas had additional observers (LFN members and their friends or relatives) who helped out on one, several or on many occasions. These included: Mike Darney, Trudy Estok, Anthea Farr, Al Grass, Lori Gurr, Jake Harris, Liam Henderson, Adeline & Karen Nicol, Mary Rempel, Stewart Sendall, Ed Sing, Karen Wiebe, Ron Wilmshurst, and Eunice Wilson. Data analysis for initial reports was done by Dan's son, biologist Rob Rempel, and data visualization was done by Michael Gluck.

A Cast of 10 Stars

What birds were counted? Ten species were tallied in each area:

1. Bald Eagle
2. Red-tailed Hawk
3. Rough-legged Hawk
4. Northern Harrier
5. Sharp-shinned Hawk
6. Cooper's Hawk
7. Peregrine Falcon
8. Merlin
9. American Kestrel
10. Northern Shrike*

All of these species are charismatic, with piercing eyes and gorgeous feathers, smooth or ruffled. Many of them are also beneficial to farmers, keeping rodents and other crop pests in check.

Although technically a songbird, the Northern Shrike was included because it behaves like a small raptor.

Clockwise: Bald Eagle, Red-tailed Hawk, Northern Harrier.
Photos: John Gordon

The Numbers and What They Tell Us

How many were counted? Over the 26 years, in the three areas combined, 8,814 individuals were recorded. Red-tailed Hawks dominated (63.8% of all observations), with Bald Eagles placing second (25.3% of all observations). The remaining eight species placed as follows: **3)** Northern Harrier (4.5%), **4)** Cooper's Hawk (2.4%), **5)** Northern Shrike (1.4%), **6)** Rough-legged Hawk (1.0%), **7)** Sharp-shinned Hawk (0.6%), **8)** American Kestrel (0.5%), **9)** Peregrine Falcon (0.3%) and **10)** Merlin (0.2%).

Which area had the most? That depends which species you look at. Red-tailed Hawks were evenly distributed across all three areas, with an average number per monthly survey of 12.5 in Area A, 12.3 in Area B and 12.7 in Area C. These numbers are astoundingly close, which suggests that Red-tailed Hawks are adaptable (not too fussy) about their choice of habitat.

Comparisons between areas for the three most abundant raptor species.

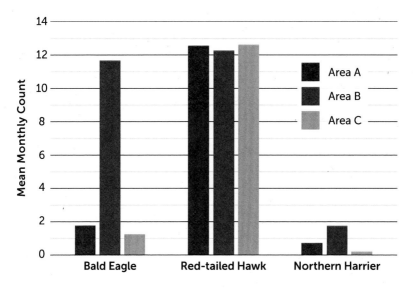

In contrast, Bald Eagles clearly excelled in Area B, which is to be expected as this area lies next to the Fraser River. The third most common raptor, the Northern Harrier, also had the highest average number per monthly survey in Area B.

The other seven raptor species all had an average number per monthly survey of below one. Again, Area B scored higher than other areas, with one exception. The exception was the Rough-legged Hawk, which had a higher monthly average in Area A. Overall, Area B was the "winner", providing the best habitats for the most raptors.

Were there trends or cycles? Bald Eagles certainly did increase from their very low numbers in the early 1980s. But in the last decade there were large fluctuations. Highest population peaks occurred in Area B, in March 1998 (143), March 2000 (110) and Feb 2004 (120). One of the take-away messages from the LFN Raptor Count is that long-term counts of raptors are essential for a clearer picture of what is going on. A single count could occur in a "peak" or in a "valley" and lead to misleading conclusions.

Rough-legged Hawk. Photo: John Gordon

Peak counts of Bald Eagles in each area.

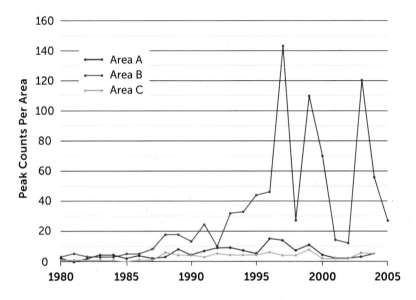

Like the eagles, Red-tailed Hawks also showed large fluctuations in peak numbers. Perhaps the lower numbers seen near the end of the count (as noted by Ray in 2005) were due to habitat loss. In Glen Valley, some large pastures (where Red-tailed Hawks hunted for voles) were converted to more lucrative blueberry and cranberry farms.

It is difficult to find population trends in the other raptor species because they occurred in low numbers. We do know that Rough-legged hawks, most common in Area A, were seen there less frequently as the years progressed.

Of note were two other rarer raptor species recorded during the counts. A Northern Goshawk was seen in Area C in 1994 and a Short-eared Owl was recorded eight times in Area B between 1985 and 2000.

A Short-eared Owl was occasionally seen during the search for eagles, hawks, and falcons. Photo: John Gordon

The Bigger Picture

How does all this fit into the bigger picture? The LFN Raptor Count provides a valuable window back in time, when Langley and Surrey were more rural and less busy. Sadly, the chances of spotting either a Short-eared Owl or a Rough-legged Hawk are even smaller than they were during the Raptor Count. The Short-eared Owl has declined across Canada, so much so that it is now listed as Threatened by COSEWIC (the Committee on the Status of Endangered Wildlife in Canada). Based on Christmas Bird Counts, Rough-legged Hawks have also declined elsewhere in the Lower Mainland, such as Delta, where greenhouses have replaced many open fields. Yet in other parts of North America, their numbers appear to be stable—thankfully.

The increase in Bald Eagles after the mid-1980s was widespread. The species is described as a conservation success story, with populations recovering across the continent. Such a recovery was mainly due to the phasing out of DDT in the mid-1970s (DDT is a potent pesticide which also causes egg shell thinning), plus the ending of the bounty that was placed on eagles by the Alaskan government from 1917 to 1953.

Of the species chosen for the LFN Raptor Count, only one (in 2022) is listed as a BC species at risk: the Peregrine Falcon. In Canada, COSEWIC lists the Peregrine as a species of Special Concern. The concern, provincially and federally, comes from the falcon's low numbers.

Overall populations of the other nine LFN Raptor Count species are currently thought to be stable or of least concern in North America. However, three of these should perhaps have small "warning flags" beside them. The Northern Harrier, American Kestrel and the Northern Shrike have shown long-term declines in some areas, particularly in eastern North America. Citizen science can continue to play an important role in monitoring these and other raptor populations.

Peregrine Falcon. Photo: John Gordon

The Threats

What dangers do raptors face? There are many human-caused threats facing eagles, hawks, falcons and owls. These include habitat loss (for nesting, foraging, perching, roosting), pesticides (such as rat poison), collisions with high voltage power lines, collisions with cars, ingestion of lead shot (in waterfowl or in carrion), being shot or wounded (illegal hunting) and human disturbance (at nest sites).

For ground-nesting raptors such as Northern Harriers, dogs are a threat near urban areas. Bald Eagles face additional threats in the marine environment from oil spills or entanglement with fishing gear. Climate change is another looming threat, particularly for Rough-legged Hawks which nest in the Arctic, feeding mainly on lemmings on the tundra. In other areas, climate change has already brought wildfires and heat waves that have been deadly, especially to nestlings.

On the Plus Side...

Currently in Langley, we can be glad that there is still a good variety of raptors to be found, thanks to farmland and fields and forests and streams still existing and still mostly healthy. Thanks also to the adaptability of certain raptors. We are lucky—so far.

Our hope is that with careful, long-term municipal and regional planning, we can prevent future losses of habitat, thus ensuring that these charismatic and important birds remain an integral part of our landscape.

Are there still surprises? Yes, yes and yes! Langley still has surprises: a Golden Eagle in north Langley (2022), a Great Gray Owl in north Langley (2022) and the jaw-dropping discovery of a Snowy Owl in a Douglas-fir tree in central Langley (2017, during the Christmas Bird Count).

There are moments when naturalists feel a deep connection with nature, when time stands still, when the cold or the rain or the snow no longer matter. When your eyes suddenly, unexpectedly, meet the eyes of a hawk or an eagle or an owl (that has probably been watching you for some time). Yes, that can be one such moment.

A close-up view of a Short-eared Owl in a February snowstorm. The Raptor Count became one of the focal points—an element of cohesion—that strengthened the club and helped keep it together. Members knew that it was something to be proud of. Photo: John Gordon

CHAPTER 10

Education:
Learning at Any Age

by Anthea Farr & Anne Gosse

It's darker than Hades, I'm thinking. We are crawling along the ground, underneath shrubs, at night—possibly the darkest night possible. Clouds have obscured any chance of moonlight or starlight. I'm in a long procession of "crawlers"; the boy ahead of me is dressed entirely in black. I can't see him at all. *What madness is this?*

A twig snaps and we all freeze. And listen. I hear the soft patter of rain drops on the leaves above, then the rustle of someone's jacket. The rich scent of damp earth, damp ferns, damp salmonberry, is getting stronger. Under my left hand, the moss feels ever so soft. *What madness is this?* I know the answer. Naturalists should learn to use all their senses to better understand nature...

— **ANTHEA FARR: NATUREKIDS CAMP, GOLDEN EARS**

Long before an organization called NatureKids (aka Young Naturalists) was created in BC, the LFN was engaged in many other types of nature education. Right from the outset, educational programs have been presented at our monthly meetings.

Educational Programs

For the first few decades, these programs took the form of slide shows, with Kodachrome, Fujichrome or Ektachrome slides placed carefully into a slide carousel, which was then carefully placed into a slide projector. Then, slide by slide, the carousel rotated. Few young folks today will be familiar with this process!

Facing: Anne Gosse with mossy beard. Photo: Anthea Farr

Times changed and we moved on to memory sticks and Power-Point presentations, with a PowerPoint projector. Then came the pandemic. In-person programs had to shift to Zoom presentations. This had some negatives but it also had some positives.

One big advantage was that we could now invite biologists and other fabulous presenters who lived far away (even in the U.S.A.) to give us programs. Our current program coordinator, Anne Gosse, took full advantage of this new opportunity. We were treated to a fascinating variety of programs, with topics such as whales, wolves, sturgeon, green roofs and living walls.

Sometimes our own members also gave programs via Zoom, from comfortable quarters at home. Topics have included local nature and far-flung travels. To increase viewership, colourful informative posters were made and sent with emails to members and to other clubs to remind them about upcoming programs. We are much indebted to Anne and to all previous program coordinators for 50 years of illustrated talks that enlightened, inspired and entertained.

Community Education

Our membership has often included individual members who have felt inspired or emboldened to teach others about nature. One such individual was Irene Pearce, a retired teacher, who enjoyed giving nature talks or leading nature-orientated field trips for elementary school kids.

Other members did the same for Sparks, Brownies, Guides, Beavers, Cubs or Scouts. For example, for several years Joan Taylor (LFN Secretary) and Anne Gosse (then LFN Field Trips Coordinator) led groups of Langley Girl Guides, Brownies and Sparks on nature walks in our local parks. As well as helping

Leading Girl Guides on a nature walk. Photo: LFN Archives

the girls to learn about birds, flowers and trees, they helped Girl Guides find their "required 12 birds" so that they could earn their Birdwatching Badges.

Other individuals have been more comfortable giving slide-illustrated nature talks at Seniors' community centers or at local libraries. Then there are those volunteers who have manned the LFN booth at community events. This invariably results in chatting to visitors of all sorts and ages, usually educating them about nature in the process.

NatureKids

When NatureKids Nicomekl was formed in 2003, LFN's focus on nature education shifted to include that group. This focus was shared by the White Rock & Surrey Naturalists, as "Nicomekl" included both Langley and Surrey. As a co-leader, I was lucky to have a succession of excellent and knowledgeable co-leaders: Tineke Goebertus and then Lynn Pollard from the White Rock &

Surrey Naturalists; Sarah Brookes, Chantelle DesLauriers, and Angie Grant from Surrey Parks; and educator Jenny Pollard, Lynn's daughter.

We were also fortunate to be able to draw on superb naturalist volunteers to lead our explorer days: Al Grass (spiders, bugs), John Gordon (photography), Sheila Puls (sheep farming), Phil Henderson (bog botany), Tom Bearss (birdwatching), Terry Taylor (fungi), Carlo Giovanella (geology)—and so many more!

How can I forget our Houston Trail walk, when a boy caught a large beetle, bright red all over and totally amazing? Of course, Al Grass knew right away what it was (a net-winged beetle) and told us all interesting facts about it. Al's enthusiasm for nature, especially insects and spiders, definitely filtered down into these young minds.

Early on, my co-leader, Lynn, and I decided to boldly go where no Lower Mainland club had gone before. We would offer an annual long weekend camp for our NatureKids families. This way we could immerse kids in nature for three days and three nights. We succeeded, wildly, with the camp becoming so popular that a waiting list often had to be created.

To immerse the kids in different habitats, we booked group sites in different provincial parks: Deas Island, Golden Ears, Manning, Skagit, Alice Lake, Green Lake, Porpoise Bay, Miracle Beach. Happily, the Langley Field Naturalists and White Rock & Surrey Naturalists agreed to subsidize these camps, which kept camp costs low for each family.

Our camp programs always included night walks and star gazing, campfires, lively nature games, birdwatching walks, nature arts and crafts, and—most challenging of all—"Botany or Bust". The latter was an effort to teach kids about native plants, knowledge that seemed to be sorely lacking.

At first it was a struggle, but with time, strategies evolved that seemed to work. As well as plant names, we talked about how our native plants were used by First Nations and which ones could be eaten. We used repetition and we used candy. "Botany or Bust" culminated with each child being individually tested. Points were awarded for correct answers (helpful clues were sometimes given, especially for younger members). The more points scored, the more candies were doled out.

Imagine how pleased we were to learn later that some of our NatureKids were teaching their school classmates or their friends about native plants. We had made ripples in the void of native plant education!

Another positive outcome of the camps was bonding. The kids at camp sometimes formed long-lasting friendships; ditto for the adults (parents or grandparents) at camp. There is nothing quite like chopping wood, roasting marshmallows, paddling canoes, hiking mountain trails, belting out camp songs—or going on the *notorious* night walks—to really get to know each other.

What does the future hold for LFN's nature education? Clearly, there will always be a need and a desire for it. The next 50 years may contain some surprises, but we are sure that educating ourselves and other folks about nature will remain a worthwhile endeavour.

NatureKids meeting a garter snake.
Photo: Anthea Farr

CHAPTER 11

The Social Side of Things: Fun and Camaraderie

by Nora Truman & Anthea Farr

"In the early years, there were cakes. Not just to celebrate the club's significant anniversaries (such as 5th or 10th). No, instead we celebrated the club with a cake every year. Of course, this was not just about eating, but rather an excuse—any excuse will do—to gather, have fun and socialize." — **ANTHEA FARR**

Then and Now

The social side of the LFN has changed little over five decades. Our meeting place has changed from the old to the new music school, but the sound of laughter may still greet you as you approach the meeting room. This laughter may mingle with the sound of plates of savories and sweets being dropped off and placed on a table. You might also catch a delicious aroma, as pots of coffee and tea begin to brew.

You could notice that our dress is casual, perhaps augmented by some bling or a special hat to celebrate a season or occasion. Before the meeting begins, you might visit the lending library, a

Facing: Toots Tucker having fun with a butterfly hat at the Campbell Valley Butterfly Tea Party. Beside her is Esther Johnson of the White Rock and Surrey Naturalists. Photo: Metro Vancouver file photo
Above: LFN President Lisa Dreves with Sheila Puls, ready to cut the LFN 50th Anniversary cakes. Photo: Bob Puls

busy place with members browsing the various books on birds, butterflies, plants, etc., not only from our area but from all over the world. Then the greeting table by the door will grow quiet as folks settle in for the meeting, anticipating a chat and snack afterwards. As always, we strive to make these meetings fun, educational, and welcoming. More about the "nature" of our educational programs is described in Chapter 10.

Outdoor picnics have also been common throughout the LFN's existence. Not just a chance to study ants, picnics provide an opportunity to share sightings and knowledge and to get to know fellow naturalists better. The summer potluck picnic at the Grass Shack (the home of Al and Jude Grass) was always much anticipated. Feasting would be followed by birding or plant or mushroom identification on the nearby trails, with Al Grass as the leader.

Members flocking together to carry the LFN banner.
Left to right: Brenda Code, Rhys Griffiths, Arnold and Wilma Chadney
Photo: LFN Archives

Top: 2019. Socializing after the Christmas Bird Count.
Photo: LFN Archives
Bottom: 2021. LFN gathering at Campbell Valley Park.
Photo: Anne Gosse

Even when downright chilly, socializing has continued. Following winter field trips, members have often congregated in warming huts or in coffee shops. Over lunch or a snack, sightings have been shared and discussed (sometimes disputed) in cozy surroundings.

Then came the pandemic. Forced to adapt to pandemic restrictions, from late 2019 to late 2022 we had Zoom presentations instead of in-person meetings. Even so, we still at times sported some funny hats of the season. Summer was no problem; we had our outdoor picnics, socially distancing in the vast meadows of Campbell Valley Park.

Socializing on a Wider Scale

As a member of BC Nature, the Langley Field Naturalists can easily connect with other naturalists across the province. The best example of this is at BC Nature's Annual General Meeting, hosted by a different club in a different part of BC each year. Besides socializing and exploring different natural environments, attendees learn about other clubs' successful endeavours to protect nature.

Meeting and Greeting

Naturally, some naturalists are more social than others. Here we profile two of our members who are exceptionally good at meeting and greeting: Sylvia Anderson and Toots (Gertrude) Tucker. First, let's listen in on one of their conversations…

Crack, Snap – Ouch!
"What was that?"
"I think a garter snake just disappeared under that rock."
"Sorry Toots," says Sylvia, "I thought this was the new path to the Nature House. We better turn back."
The two ladies climb back along the rugged path and follow the main trail for their shift at the Nature House, in Campbell Valley Regional Park.
"Don't forget to show the visitors the ant hill today,"
says Sylvia. "It is getting really huge and amazing."
"I know," says Toots with her big smile.

Sylvia Anderson, a dedicated volunteer. Photo: Elly McNeilly

This conversation reveals two things: 1) they are committed to reaching their destination and fulfilling their volunteer duties, and 2) they both enjoy showing or talking about nature to others. Such individuals, with their smiles and warm greetings, are often the most important members of a club. As well as showing ant hills to park visitors, Sylvia and Toots have excelled at welcoming visitors to LFN meetings.

Sylvia has worn "many hats", including LFN President and Metro Vancouver's Coordinator and trainer of volunteer Nature House hosts. Toots has been volunteering for many organizations in Langley since 1953. She has been an example and friend for hosts of the Nature House who are just learning the ropes. She also served as the LFN librarian for many years, inviting members and visitors to borrow books about nature at our general meetings.

These two exemplary club volunteers often work together and have been greeters at our LFN display booth on many occasions: at Rivers Day in Williams Park, Country Celebration at Campbell Valley Regional Park, Heritage Apple Day at Derby Reach Regional Park, and Langley Community Day in Douglas Park.

We thank all of the meeters and greeters who have served our club over the past half century!

50 Years Strong and Beyond

by Lisa Dreves & Joanne Rosenthal

Fifty years may feel like the blink of an eye but for a non-profit organization it is more than a few lifetimes. With recent losses of sister naturalist groups, it is even more apparent that the LFN is a very strong group and an important part of BC's naturalist community. How has LFN stayed strong?

The fabric of this organization has always been flexible and fluid. Looking back on meeting minutes and lovingly prepared newsletters, we see an organization that has always been supportive, full of members who are incredibly generous with their precious time and their willingness to help fellow members with ideas others might think are completely off the wall. Many members have radiated positivity and enthusiasm that have encouraged others, including those of the next generations, to appreciate nature.

Our conservation successes also helped us stay strong. These successes relied heavily on education. As noted in Chapter 1, LFN was founded by individuals who educated the public and politicians about an important natural area and the need to conserve it: the land now called Campbell Valley Regional Park.

Over many years, we developed "recipes" for conservation success. The ingredients often included the following: conducting inventories, working with other groups, working with local governments, being proactive (such as bringing grant money to the table). These techniques served us well with Brydon Lagoon, Forslund-Watson, the Irene Pearce Trail and a host of other conservation initiatives.

Sometimes it was necessary to be that thorn in the side of local governments, but we like to think we did so with courtesy and respect. Being a member of BC Nature was also key to our success; we received support and our voice was amplified, especially with province-wide issues. Thanks to BC Nature, clubs were able to easily connect with each other, sometimes becoming powerful allies.

The next 50 years needs the LFN and all who care about nature. We find ourselves at the beginning of a new normal; hard choices need to be made to ensure a viable future for our natural environment. Those who care are growing in number but so too are the challenges. By continuing to adapt and evolve, LFN plans to attract new members, young and old(er), to share the enjoyment of nature and help protect what we love.

Lastly, we wish to give thanks to all who have come before us. Over the last 50 years, we have lost many members, relocating to new places on this earth and beyond, places from which they may be unable to return for a visit. Each member has left us changed for the better, from a kind word of encouragement after a meeting to offering a backyard to breed beetles for an entire summer. Or perhaps we have been left with a memory of a fine summer's day of camaraderie, reflection and rejoicing in nature.

"To the next 50 years, may the dawn chorus never disappoint, may our natural areas remain diverse, and may we never take fresh air for granted."

- LISA DREVES, LFN PRESIDENT

Photo: Elly McNeilly

The Big Thank You

A big **THANK YOU** to all who served in **executive roles or other positions** in the LFN over the past 50 years. Listed below in alphabetical order, these include:

Laura Addinall	Kitsy Fraser
Sylvia Anderson	Vera Frisby
Bruce Angus	Lilianne Fuller
Gerald Arthur	Eva Gibson
Jenny & Ben Auxier	Lesley Goodbrand
Gail Blair	Cecelia Gorsuch
Marjorie Buchanan	Ted Goshulak
Fred Bunnell	Anne Gosse
Ann Carmichael	Peggy Grant
Arnold & Wilma Chadney	Al & Jude Grass
Keith & Belinda Chrystall	Rhys & Annabel Griffiths
Peggy & Hubie Clarke	Alistair Grogan
June Cleghorn	Ray Gurr
Don Clisch	Eric Habisch
Dorothy Code	Phil Henderson
Arnold & Ethel Code	Donna Hill
Brenda Code	Bruce Hutchison
Tessie Copeman	Bill Image
Dorothy Danielson	Cecily Isler
Judy & Mike Darney	Ursula Kernig
Emma De Hulu	Jessie Kilby
Irene Derksen	Ruth Kirk
Lisa Dreves	Hilda Klein
John & Kathleen Ellens	Bill Knowlson
Anthea Farr	Robin Lam

Gerry Langtry	Keith Robertson
Jean & Jack Liddle	Joanne Rosenthal
Lynda Lightfoot	Glenn Ryder
Jenn Ling	Johanna Saaltink
Kay Lotzer	Sharon Sabourin/McVeigh
Kathy Masse	Ed Sing
Mary McGilliviny	Cora Surcon
Karen McNeilly	Joan & Ian Taylor
Martin McNicholl	Valerie Terpsma
Yvonne Miles	Joan Thomlinson
Natalie Minunzie	Helen Thompson
Nanny Mulder ten Kate	Phyllis Tindale
Diana Munday	Rebecca Tin Tun
Betty Mussett	Nora Truman
Adeline & Dan Nicol	Toots Tucker
Evelyn Oberg	Carol Turtle
Mike Odell	Ryan Usenik
Judy Parkman	Pat Walker
Mary & Trudy Pastrick	Jane Wallace
Irene Pearce	Sharon Ward
Janne Perrin	Tom Wildeboer
Caren Porter	Gudrun Williamson
Gareth Pugh	Joan & Ron Wilmshurst
Bob & Sheila Puls	Eunice Wilson
Dan & Mary Rempel	Gail Wool
Hywel Roberts	Pat Yeomans

We also say **THANK YOU** to a great many LFN members
who helped the club in other ways over the past 50 years:
doing field work, leading field trips, presenting programs,
working at booths, etc. **We appreciate all of you!**

LFN Publications

BOOKS
Birds of Langley
Plants of Langley
Wild about Wild Plants (children's activity book)
On the Trail: 50 Years of Engaging with Nature

PAMPHLETS
Langley Field Naturalists
Brydon Lagoon
Birds of Langley
Butterflies of Langley

REPORTS
Report on the Nature Park at The Redwoods Golf Course (2008)

Mountain View Leased Crown Land: Bio-inventory Report (2009-2018)

CHECKLISTS
Birds of Campbell Valley Regional Park

For more information or for free downloads, visit
www.langleyfieldnaturalists.org

Committee Acknowledgment

by Bob Puls & Lilianne Fuller, Project Coordinators

As the 50th anniversary of the Langley Field Naturalists approached, and knowing that we still had some founding and long-term members around whose memories could be jogged, I (Bob) suggested that we document the club's history.

A committee was convened and as things progressed, the writing morphed from dry, historical documentation to a more lively and engaging text. We had plenty of material to draw upon: archives containing minutes of all meetings (through both good and turbulent times), most of the club's newsletters, binders of information on club projects, scrapbooks containing photos and newspaper clippings, and boxes of old photographic slides.

On the Trail is a history of the club, its members, its struggles and its victories, distilled through many meetings and much work. Committee members should be proud of this work. We are grateful to all of them for their time and effort.

We hope that the pioneering work of the LFN serves as an inspiration and an invitation to young people to *know nature and keep it worth knowing.*

COMMITTEE MEMBERS:
Bob Puls, Anthea Farr, Phil Henderson, John Gordon,
Nora Truman, Kathy Masse, Joanne Rosenthal,
Gertrude (Toots) Tucker, Lisa Dreves and Lilianne Fuller.